AEROS

BY

Copyright © 1997 Omnibus Press (A Division of Book Sales Limited)

Edited by Chris Charlesworth
Cover & Book designed by 4i
Picture research by Nikki Russell

ISBN 0.7119.5598.0 Order No.OP47830

Exclusive Distributors:
Book Sales Limited, 8/9 Frith Street, London W1V 5TZ, UK.
Music Sales Corporation, 257 Park Avenue South, New York, NY 10010, USA.
Music Sales Pty Limited, 120 Rothschild Avenue, Rosebery, NSW 2018, Australia.

To the Music Trade only:
Music Sales Limited, 8/9 Frith Street, London W1V 5TZ, UK.

Photo credits:
front cover; LFI. All other pictures supplied by LFI and Barry Plummer.
Every effort has been made to trace the copyright holders of the photographs in this book but one or two were unreachable.
We would be grateful if the photographers concerned would contact us.

Printed in the United Kingdom by Ebenezer Baylis & Son, Worcester.

A catalogue record for this book is available from the British Library.

OMNIBUS PRESS
LONDON · NEW YORK · SYDNEY

CONTENTS

INTRODUCTION

In keeping with Aerosmith's 'don't bore us, get us to the chorus' attitude, I'm going to try and keep this introduction as short as possible. This book is primarily concerned with Aerosmith's recorded career – the albums, what went into them and, most importantly, the songs that came out. It is not a biography, and nor is it intended to be. However, links in theme have been made to ensure continuity and when important events have occurred within the group's life, they are mentioned.

Briefly, Aerosmith are Steven Tyler (vocals), Joe Perry (lead guitar and backing vocals), Brad Whitford (lead guitar), Tom Hamilton (bass) and Joey Kramer (drums). Formed in New Hampshire, Boston, USA in 1970 and taking blues, funk and British invaders The Yardbirds and The Beatles as their musical blueprint, Aerosmith have subsequently become one of America's most successful and enduring rock acts, selling in excess of 25 million albums and garnering immense critical acclaim for their songs and spirited live performances.

In a career spanning nearly three decades, they have encountered fame, drugs, near-disintegration and, most surprisingly, a comeback from the dead that many thought impossible.

Vernon Reid, ex-guitarist from the much missed Living Colour describes them thus, 'Aerosmith have a unique sound somewhere between the Stones and Led Zeppelin. They're one of the last great bands of the Seventies that forged the bridge between heavy rock and r&b.'

Getting back to the songs. After listening to their entire catalogue for the thousandth time, I'm no nearer to understanding what imbues Aerosmith with their peculiar magic. Like many, I have my theories; the 'dynamic' tension between Perry's guitar and Tyler's voice; the way Whitford and Hamilton lock into Kramer's snare; the 'voodoo' of that dragged beat. God, it might even be their sense of humour. But in the cold light of day, I'm as lost as the next man. Aerosmith simply 'swagger' and that's it.

Nonetheless, it's been a great pleasure trying to capture their essence and I can only hope that reading about the songs leads you to play them.

Numbers given refer to CD releases, unless stated otherwise.

Martin Power, August 1996

THE COLUMBIA YEARS
AEROSMITH

AEROSMITH (ORIGINAL RELEASE: JANUARY 1973; CD RELEASE COLUMBIA/CBS 4666662)

Joe Perry: 'You didn't get a record contract if you were a rock band that lived in Boston. You had to go to New York and audition.'

Aerosmith were signed to Columbia Records in August 1972 by the then president of the company, Clive Davis. Impressed by a demo sent to him by Leber-Krebs, the band's management company, Davis took a chance and ventured to Max's Kansas City, a lower Manhattan rock club, to see them perform a showcase set. Suitably entranced by their combination of raw blues and youthful arrogance, legend has it that he made them a tentative offer that very night, quietly uttering the words, 'Yes, I think we can do something with you.'

That 'something' turned out to be a major recording contract, worth reportedly, the then princely sum of $125,000. Nevertheless, the group would have to work hard for their money, producing two albums a year, and in a convoluted back door deal, donating a large slice of any profits generated to their management. Green as apples and just eager to get the ball rolling, Aerosmith raised no objections. Taking a modest slice of the advance to book themselves studio time, the band were to begin work on their début LP within weeks.

The venue chosen for recording was Boston's Intermedia Sound, 'A real Frankenstein's lab of a place,' according to Tom Hamilton, 'With a mixing desk that looked like it was made of cardboard with knobs the size of car headlamps.' Yet to the inexperienced musicians, it was an Aladdin's Cave full of possibilities, brimming with toys – and besides, it was within budget.

As was the man chosen to produce and co-engineer the inaugural effort,

Adrian Barber. A young talent whose credits included work with The Allman Brothers, Vanilla Fudge and Cream, his brief was simple – to capture the energy that Clive Davis had seen that night.

Steaming ahead with little regard for vagaries such as food and sleep, Aerosmith were to complete the record within an astonishing (by today's standards) two weeks – including a period of re-recording/mixing supervised by additional producer Ray Colcord. Nonetheless, the process had been considerably aided by the group choosing to record songs already in their live set, thus cutting down on costly rehearsal and arrangement time. 'We'd played the songs many, many times,' said Hamilton, 'And we were all fired up to lay them down.'

The result, released in January 1973 (and wrapped in a rather hippie cover with Aerosmith looking like the cast of *Hair*) was a primitive blues rock LP, heavy on attitude, and with occasional flashes of brilliance. Sounding rough and ready, Barber had elected largely to go for a live sound with minimum frills, and though not particularly radio friendly, it suited the songs' honest charm well.

Setting a precedent for the future, Tyler's name was on all but one cut (the cover of Rufus Thomas' 'Walkin' The Dog'), but evidence of the growing partnership between the singer and guitarist Joe Perry was also present with the backwater blues of 'Movin' Out'. However, for the moment, Steven had provided the album's stand outs with 'Dream On', 'Mama Kin' and 'One Way Street' all destined for classic status.

The group were reasonably happy with their accomplishment. 'When the album came out, we started to own Boston,' commented Tyler. Yet when sales peaked at 40,000 (their New England audience), any nascent hopes of overnight international success were crushed. Beginning a tortuous cycle of 'tour, record, tour, record' that would only end in 1979 (and at great personal cost to them), Aerosmith hit the road to promote the LP. Still, the single 'Dream On' was starting to pick up radio play, and they had at least one supporter in the press, with

Creem magazine's Dan De Witt. 'I like this band,' he declared, 'because they seem to know themselves; there's no imitation country or superhip posturing... just a few pimples and a full LP of screaming, metallic, creative rock and roll.' Unfortunately, it would be a little while longer before everyone shared his view.

MAKE IT
(Tyler)

A ragged, yet assured slice of bluesy rock and roll, 'Make It' is as good a choice as any to kick off Aerosmith's recorded career. Penned by Tyler, the lyrics outline his aspirations for stardom, the song's title acting as a mantra to future success. The band work hard, infusing the track with a slow-burn feel which climaxes as it hits the last chorus. Mind you, they'd had long enough to get it right. 'Make It' had been Aerosmith's set-opener for some time. Bassist Tom Hamilton summed up the number's appeal well, 'Our first song from our first album... just a great way to get things going.'

SOMEBODY
(Tyler, Emspack)

Another Tyler composition, though this time co-assisted by his old friend Steven Emspack, 'Somebody' is the album's weakest moment. Based on a chugging, bone dry guitar riff which never really gets out of the starting blocks, the song's highlight is a lead guitar/vocal duet which recalls either George Benson or Deep Purple, depending on your preference.

DREAM ON
(Tyler)

The first great Aerosmith song, and still as emotional and fulfilling today as it was in 1973. Written by Steven Tyler on his father's piano at the tender age of seventeen, 'Dream On' is a poignant and lyrically mature power ballad, arguably as important in rock's development as Zeppelin's 'Stairway To Heaven' or Lynyrd Skynyrd's 'Freebird'.

From its gentle, neo-classical Bach-style opening, all descending minor chords and picked sensitivity, to its roaring, open-throated climax, the song is sheer class and gave a clear indication to all concerned that the group were more than a bargain basement Rolling Stones copy – a criticism that would unfairly follow Aerosmith for much of their recorded life.

Released as a single at the time, 'Dream On' would only go as high as No.59 in the US charts, causing its writer considerable pain, as he knew its true worth. However, Tyler would have the last laugh as, three years later, with Aerosmith having cracked America wide open, it would be re-released, this time scaling the Top 10 to No.6, and proving a point to his cohort Tom Hamilton, who had regularly woken to the song's haunting refrain when the band had shared an apartment together. 'My room was the only room big enough to put a piano in. So, I woke up every morning to Steven playing this weird song in the key of F, telling me how much of a hit it would be – and it turned out to be 'Dream On'.

Forever a highlight on their concert set, fans still flick their cigarette lighters

from producing a magnificent solo when Aerosmith performed the song live with a 60-piece orchestra for MTV's 10th Anniversary some years ago – although the look of surprise as his cohort Tyler flew over his head at the keys of a grand piano, suspended by a crane – was priceless.

ONE WAY STREET
(Tyler)

Jazz-inflected, and mining a deep, danceable groove, 'One Way Street' sees Aerosmith moving away from the more traditional rock formula, but without losing an ounce of their power. Driven along with military precision by drummer Joey Kramer – 'I can remember (bassist) Tom and me drilling on the 'One Way Street' shuffle until we drove the old lady downstairs crazy' – and given a light, strutting bounce by Hamilton's bass work, the track nevertheless remains a showcase for Tyler's remarkable talents. Voice raw as sandpaper, the frontman takes hold of his song and simply lets rip, burning down

on in a show of solidarity to the track's key prophetic phrase, 'You got to lose to know how to win'. Yet, it has always been privately rumoured that guitarist Joe Perry doesn't much care for the number, seeing it as getting in the way of his preference for the band's rockier moments. Nevertheless, it didn't seem to stop him the melody line like a young James Brown, adding angry, unrestrained harmonica fills to accentuate his overall authority. Only Perry comes close to stealing the limelight from his singer, with a drunken, free-falling solo that trademarks many of the moves the guitarist would become famous for. Played live early in their career, Aerosmith would put the song in mothballs for much of the Eighties, before dragging it screaming back into life for their legendary Marquee performance in 1990 – only to inexplicably drop it again for the 'Get A Grip' tour. Pity.

MAMA KIN
(Tyler)

Another subsequent classic, 'Mama Kin' is a simple Stones-inspired rocker, which Steven brought with him to the band, and Aerosmith made their own. An everyday tale of, 'Sleepin' late and smokin' tea', the track humorously chronicles Tyler's pursuit of the rock and roll lifestyle (a discipline in which he would become notably proficient) and features superb performances from each member of the group. It also introduces a horn solo – courtesy of saxophonist David Woodford – to their sound which proves a match made in heaven. Skittering gypsy beat, hook line and sinker chorus, and Perry and Woodford dovetailing in and out of the main riff with fighter pilot-like efficiency, it's all here. Tyler loved the song so much he had a tattoo bearing its name embedded permanently into his upper left arm. 'I was so proud of that tune that I figured it would live forever one way or another – on my flesh if not in the record books!'

Much played on US FM radio to this day, and still sporadically gracing their live concerts, 'Mama Kin' remains inspirational. It certainly was to rock giants in the making, Guns N' Roses, who included a spirited cover of the tune on their début EP 'Live ?!*@ Like A Suicide'.

WRITE ME A LETTER
(Tyler)

A catchy bar-room boogie, graced with some tasty harmonica and guitar flourishes, this track threatens to really warm up in its middle section with a clever switch in both key and mood, but before we know it, we're back into the verse, and safer waters. Pleasant enough, but not a patch on the last three cuts.

MOVIN' OUT
(Tyler, Perry)

Inspired by a notice of eviction served on the band at their shared apartment on Commonwealth Avenue, Boston, 'Movin' Out' is notable as the first musical collaboration between Joe Perry and Steven Tyler. A moody slice of proto-blues rock, it may now seem ragged and undisciplined compared to their later efforts. However, given its gut-bucket riffing and authentic under-rehearsed feel, the song does retain a certain down at heel charm that proves difficult not to wallow in.

WALKIN' THE DOG
(Thomas)

Written by Rufus Thomas and introduced to Aerosmith via Joey Kramer (who had spent years playing the song in various soul revues), 'Walkin' The Dog' is the only cover version from the band's then live set to grace their début album. It was also covered by the Stones on their first album way back in 1964.

Ably captured by producer Barber – who seems to temporarily step away from his 'press-record' approach, opting instead to experiment with various reverb and echo f/x – Aerosmith seem relaxed and at home, imbuing the track with a salty, sexually charged feel, all scratched guitars and sly, rhythmic stabs. Tyler even manages to chuck a wood flute into the proceedings, presumably to add some class to the down and dirty groove. Still sporadically played live (with the vocalist changing the lyric 'silver buttons up and down her back' to something altogether less innocent) and destined to retain its favoured status within the group, 'Walkin' The Dog' closes things very nicely here.

GET YOUR WINGS

(ORIGINAL RELEASE: MARCH 1974; CD RELEASE COLUMBIA/CBS 4667322)

Escaping the road in the autumn of 1973 to enter New York's Power Plant Studios – the choice of venue undoubtedly influenced by The Rolling Stones and Led Zeppelin's visits there – Aerosmith's second album saw the group introduce a new element to their sound which would prove vital to their future success: sophistication.

While their début had been an earthy celebration of the blues rock that so inspired them, 'Get Your Wings' was a far more rounded beast, employing the use of a full horn section to punctuate tempo, acoustic guitars to emphasise light and shade, and most importantly the studio itself. By immersing themselves in the technology available, Aerosmith's sound took a considerable leap forward into the realms of real experimentation, and thus originality.

Assuming production duties for the record were old friends Ray Colcord and Jack Douglas, supervised by 'executive producer' Bob Ezrin, whose collaborations with shock rock king Alice Cooper had resulted in the million sellers 'Billion Dollar Babies' and 'School's Out'. But though Ezrin no doubt kept a watchful eye and Colcord continued to bring ideas of his own, it was Douglas who forged a critical connection with the quintet – a connection which would last ten years and ultimately bear such sweet fruit as 'Toys In The Attic' and 'Rocks'.

Having already engineered Cooper's 'Billion Dollar Babies' and The New York Dolls' first LP, Douglas had developed a relaxed and open approach to studio work, suiting the young Aerosmith down to the ground. Eager to achieve, but disliking a military atmosphere in which to do so, his active encouragement of the group to explore new terrain was well received, and his formidable skills with song arrangement brought order to a sometimes chaotic creative process.

Though it would take another album to really throw the door wide open, the newly formed collaboration between band and producer did create four distinct gems: 'Same Old Song And Dance', 'Lord Of The Thighs', the flagship 'Train Kept A Rollin'' and the ghostly 'Seasons Of Wither'. These tunes announced a major step forward in the band's development, and broadly hinted to audiences everywhere that significant development had taken place.

'Get Your Wings', with its Jimmy lenner Jr. cover depicting a brooding group image shot in black and white (Tyler's trademark scarf packed with drugs for the session), and a formative version of the famous Aero wings logo emblazoned above their heads, was released to the world in March 1974. Backed by exhaustive touring, it sold reasonably well, shifting between 5-6,000 copies a week, subsequently floating around the middle reaches of the US album chart for some months. The LP

also put Aerosmith on national radio, spawning two FM radio hits for the singles 'Same Old Song And Dance' and 'Train Kept A Rollin''.

Even though the highly influential *Rolling Stone* magazine backed the album, declaring that it surged, 'With pent up fury', avoiding 'The excesses to which many of their peers succumb', most critics remained lukewarm, and the buzz needed to push 'Get Your Wings' to the desperately desired platinum status did not take place. Still, the campaign had made definite progress, and as Aerosmith made their way across the USA, they could take heart from one thing: Those all important little girls were beginning to understand.

SAME OLD SONG AND DANCE
(Tyler, Perry)

The first single to be released from 'Get Your Wings' and a perfect way to start any record. Based on a fuel-injected Perry Riff in E major, with Tyler 'filling the blanks', this is a classic piece of horn-driven stadium rock that, like the best wines, has seasoned with age.

Gaining its lyrical slant from, 'One girl who was pulling on my guitar player's balls', it features superb performances from all band members, though special mentions must be made for Joe's astonishingly tuneful slide solo and guest saxophonist Michael Brecker's wheezy, mid-track burn up.

Inventive, humorous and featuring the best ever use of the word 'constipation' in a rock song, 'Same Old Song & Dance' is definitely one of Aerosmith's Top 10 cuts.

LORD OF THE THIGHS
(Tyler)

'I remember we needed one more song for 'Get Your Wings' and we needed it fast. We locked ourselves into Studio C at the record plant, and this is what we came up with. I remember Steven was really psyched, and I think it shows' –Tom Hamilton.

And so was born 'Lord Of The

Thighs'. A lyrical meditation on the 'sights' of New York City, replete with double-entendres by the barrel-load, the song is actually much darker than it might at first sound. Infused with a loose, eerie structure and chord shards from Perry and Whitford cutting sporadically across Tyler's vocals, 'Thighs' sees Aerosmith experimenting with rhythm and space and proving themselves rather successful at it. Slow-burning and yet dynamic, the track would be extended into a musical free-for-all at their live shows, with Perry usually finding himself in slide-guitar

hyperspace. Check out 'Live! Bootleg''s manic performance for the proof.

SPACED
(Tyler, Perry)

Just plain odd. Perhaps Tyler had been watching too much Star Trek, but this ode to the sole survivor of a future world catastrophe really does require the listener to suspend large amounts of disbelief.

Jumping from one musical idea to another within seconds, there are some pleasing moments to be had, but the

overall impression is one of an experiment looking for a tune. Best filed under 'interesting diversion'.

WOMAN OF THE WORLD
(Tyler, Solomon)

A leftover from Tyler's pre-Aerosmith past, co-penned with former cohort Don Solomon, 'Woman Of The World' is a pleasant little rocker, switching mood and tempo several times to keep your interest piqued. Perry and Whitford make the song their own with some clever guitar interplay, and Joe even provides a brief acoustic interlude for any romantics who might be listening.

S.O.S. (TOO BAD)
(Tyler)

The heaviest track they'd laid down thus far, S.O.S. (or 'Same Old Shit' as it was more affectionately known) is a real bruiser, all sneers and cut-throat riffing. Penned by Tyler, the song remained a reliable live vehicle until it was led quietly off

to pasture in the early Eighties.

TRAIN KEPT A ROLLIN'
(Bradshaw, Mann, Kay)

Flawless. Originally written by Howie Kay, Louis Mann and Tim Bradshaw, 'T.K.A.R.' was first made famous by rockabilly act Johnny Burnette and his Rock and Roll Trio in the Fifties. However, it would come to the attention of Aerosmith via their heroes The Yardbirds, who recorded their own spirited version of the song for their 1966 LP 'Having A Rave Up...'. Yardbirds descendants Led Zeppelin opened their earliest shows with the song and returned to it occasionally throughout their entire career.

A standard they'd jammed on a thousand times in the past, Aerosmith's inclusion of 'Train' on 'Get Your Wings' is a stroke of genius. Beginning with Perry's whistle-like riff, the band lock into the beat and just don't let go. Creating a push-pull effect which drives the song along in startling fashion, Tyler adds icing to the cake with an authoritative, attacking vocal,

giving this tale of love on the tracks just the right amount of venom it needs.

And then, when you're sure it's all over, the band re-double the pace and set off again, this time backed by the (over-dubbed) cheers of a crowd. While this second take is still in fact the product of the studio, Jack Douglas' clever production ensures you are temporarily transported to the concert hall, giving Perry's screaming solos and Kramer's machine gun drumming a stamp of live authenticity. The trick would work well, with 'Train Kept A Rollin'' becoming Aerosmith's ultimate set closer, and a meltdown opportunity for band and fans alike. Clever gimmickry aside, this remains arguably the definitive cover of a blues classic.

SEASONS OF WITHER
(Tyler)
Rising out of the mists of 'Train Kept A Rollin'' comes Steven Tyler's most haunting ballad. Based around a swirling acoustic guitar figure that seems to ascend and descend endlessly, 'Seasons Of Wither' is a poignant and at times almost spiritual meditation on the passing of love. Written by the vocalist in a fit of drug-assisted depression one Hallowe'en evening, the song is a million miles from the usual Aerosmith fayre, with a sense of dark introspection more likely found on a David Sylvian record. Mature, beguiling, and immaculately performed, it sees the band stretching their boundaries in admirable fashion.

PANDORA'S BOX
(Tyler, Kramer)
Memorable as being drummer Joey Kramer's first excursion into songwriting, 'Pandora's Box' is a slight, albeit likeable, slice of politically incorrect boogie. With Tyler back in more familiar lyrical waters (sex), some nice chordal variations of the standard blues 12-bar, and a horn section adding a sassy swing to drag the track out of that dreaded 'ordinary' status, it's a pleasant enough way to knock the album on the head.

TOYS IN THE ATTIC

(ORIGINAL RELEASE: APRIL 1975; CD RELEASE COLUMBIA/CBS 4606982)

Having toured every nook and cranny of the USA in support of 'Get Your Wings', Aerosmith were a well oiled machine when they entered New York's Record Plant for the second time in the Spring of 1975.

Spirits considerably raised by the now healthy sales of 'Wings' (500,000 and rising), and confident of the material they had written while on the road, all signs indicated that their third album might be the one to break them. It was.

Consolidating the sophistication of their previous effort and harnessing the all- important live energy of their concerts, 'Toys In The Attic''s ragged intensity cracked America open like a walnut and catapulted the band to superstar status, making them Columbia's number one artists (in front of such luminaries as Dylan and Paul Simon), as well as giving the act access to Class One Drugs !

It was thoroughly well deserved too. Retaining the services of 'Get Your Wings' engineer Jay Messina, and Jack Douglas – now in the sole producer's chair – for guidance and inspiration, Aerosmith had set about producing classic after classic in their dogged pursuit of rock immortality. 'Walk This Way', 'No More No More', 'Sweet Emotion' and the startling title track were all monsters, offering teenage America a soundtrack for the summer and a home grown alternative to British invaders Led Zeppelin and The Rolling Stones. Crucially, both Zep and the Stones were becoming ever more reclusive – touring once every two years at the most – while Aerosmith seemed to be everywhere all the time.

Even the supporting material such as 'Adam's Apple' and 'Round And Round' were a cut above their contemporaries in terms of refinement and class, and with

Perry, Whitford and Hamilton's song writing skills growing to rival Tyler's, Aerosmith had simply levelled the playing field with their own brand of hard rock and roll.

Released to rave reviews (*Creem* magazine summing the album up with the phrase 'Ohhh, bay-bee!'), and even putting the band on Top 40 AM radio thanks to the singles chart success of 'Walk This Way', 'Toys In The Attic' sprinted into the US *Billboard* chart, going gold (500,000 sales) by August 1975, and platinum (1 million sales) by year end. It would remain on the chart for another

two. Brad Whitford succinctly described the period as one of 'Everything clicking into place'.

A landmark then, 'Toys'' swaggering and humorous appeal is still fresh as a daisy some twenty years on, and serves as an abject lesson in just how good Aerosmith can be. Nonetheless, they would top it.

TOYS IN THE ATTIC
(Tyler, Perry)

Or 'Charge Of The Light Brigade', as it might be better known. This explosive

amphetamine-fuelled romp sees Jack Douglas finally capture the band's live sound on vinyl, and thus give listeners their first true understanding of the band's extraordinary natural power. With Kramer holding down a ferocious back beat, and Perry, Whitford and Hamilton simultaneously driving home the song's mammoth riff, Tyler takes us on a demented walk through his unconscious mind (his lyrical imagery here providing the inspiration for the LP's surreal cover), while still retaining his gift for melody. Fierce, and uncompromising, the controlled aural chaos of 'Toys In The Attic' would slay audiences worldwide for years to come, and inspire a plethora of young rock acts across the globe – from Def Leppard to Nirvana. R.E.M. even had the audacity to cover the tune. 'A benchmark rock and roll song for Aerosmith,' concluded Joe Perry.

UNCLE SALTY
(Tyler, Hamilton)

A brooding Beatlesque tune, narrating the descent of a little orphan girl into drugs and prostitution, 'Uncle Salty' isn't half bad, but can't hope to live up to the previous track's menacing grandeur. Still, the guitars throb (with Tom Hamilton switching to a six-string for the occasion), the vocal harmonies soar pleasingly and it's always good to find a lyric where 'pushers' rhymes with 'shovers' and doesn't sound stupid.

ADAM'S APPLE
(Tyler)

Steven's eccentric theory on the source of original sin, 'Adam's Apple' is a marvellous, bawdy rocker, never threatening for a moment to take its subject seriously. Powered along by subterranean horns and an addictive, off-kilter guitar lick, Tyler provides a screamingly funny lyric with our Eve climbing right up Adam's tree for a taste of 'Love at first bite'. Add a towering, country-inflected Perry solo for insurance, and the song never falters.

WALK THIS WAY
(Tyler, Perry)

A wise-cracking tale of lost virginity, 'Walk This Way' forever defines the word 'swagger' in the musical dictionary.

Constructed around a gorgeous Perry riff (almost ludicrous in its simplicity) and Kramer's equally straightforward rhythmic pattern, Tyler creates a hypnotic lyrical patois to accompany the resultant groove, his spicy words bouncing off the guitars and bass drum, and drilling themselves so deeply into your cerebral cortex, you'll take the song's chorus to the grave.

Released as a single, 'Walk' clambered into America's Top 10 with disarming ease, and in so doing, became the song most people associate with them. The effect was only enhanced in the mid Eighties when hard core rappers Run DMC chose to cover it (enlisting Perry and Tyler to assist them in re-creating the original magic) and scored another hit.

However, despite the radio saturation that 'Walk This Way' has enjoyed, many remain amusingly unaware of its somewhat libidinous subject matter, a fact Aerosmith's front man revels in: 'I remember reading in a newspaper, in like 1976... about how disgusting rock lyrics

are – and they used 'Walk This Way' as an example of how lyrics should be nice and wholesome... Obviously they didn't get the meaning of 'you ain't seen nothin' till you're down on the muffin'...'

BIG TEN INCH RECORD
(Weismantel)

More innuendo. An appallingly disguised hymn to the phallus (the word 'record' replacing 'dick' to avoid the censors), this big-band sounding jazzer pleases as much as it offends. Horn infested (if you'll pardon the pun) and featuring some class

harmonica and barrel-piano from Tyler and guest Scott Cushnie respectively, the band found the song (a Thirties romp) from listening to Dr Demento's radio show, and decided to include it on 'Toys In The Attic'. Filthy, sordid, but above all, funny – Aerosmith still pull 'Big Ten Inch' out live when the audience needs geeing up a bit.

SWEET EMOTION
(Tyler, Hamilton)

The first single to be pulled from 'Toys In The Attic' and still a cornerstone of

Aerosmith's concerts over twenty years on, 'Sweet Emotion' is a classic in the real sense of the word. Rising out of an almost Middle-Eastern bass hook from Tom Hamilton (allegedly inspired by a particularly fine joint he smoked) the song soon gathers pace, metamorphosing into a prime slab of good-time boogie with riffs shooting everywhere at once, but never losing their central cohesion. With a superb vocal from Tyler (his clever word play splicing between the delights of pre-pubescent flesh and his growing hatred of Joe Perry's then spouse Elissa), and a spiky, malevolent, 'What did you say about my wife' solo from Perry, 'Sweet Emotion' is all-round top stuff.

NO MORE NO MORE
(Tyler, Perry)

A bracing r&b soaked rocker, replete with emotive piano and guitar interludes, 'No More No More' features Steven Tyler's best lyrics to date. Detailing the band's rise to fame, and the attendant pressures that came with stardom, the singer's can-did admissions gave the first indication that Aerosmith were starting to feel the burn of their no-holds barred excesses: 'Times are a-changing, nothing ever stands still, If I don't start changing, I'll be writing my Will.' Drugs and alcohol were now like food and drink to the quintet, and any hopes of embracing normality were fading fast – mornings too, according to Steven, had become a fond childhood memory. 'Blood stains the ivories of my daddy's baby grand, I ain't seen the daylight since I started this band.' Whatever potential storms may have been brewing in Aerosmith's future, this number can now be seen, as Joe Perry put it, as, 'A page from our diary' and a vivid re-creation of the lifestyle in which they were then immersed.

ROUND AND ROUND
(Tyler, Whitford)

Enter Brad Whitford. While the always underrated guitarist had made some tasty contributions to the band's sound in the past, 'Round And Round' marked his arrival as a songwriter – and rather a good one at that. 'Quite a production,' as Whitford succinctly put it, the track was the heaviest thing Aerosmith had yet recorded. And though its doom-laden hook was somewhat at odds with the rest of 'Toys In The Attic''s more sprightly sound, it again highlighted the band's willingness to experiment with their sound, this time entering areas even Black Sabbath might have thought twice about. Pulsating, and soaked with malevolent intent, 'Round And Round' really does assault the eardrums, especially its ending.

The aural equivalent of the work of surrealist painter Escher, the song fades out on a steadily ascending scale, which threatens to reach the heavens before falling back into itself, only to rise again, and again. Disturbing certainly, but recommended.

YOU SEE ME CRYING
(Tyler, Solomon)

'You See Me Crying' brings the album to a close in truly orchestral fashion. A Tyler/Solomon ballad (called back into service from his Chain Reaction days), enhanced by stirring strings and sentimental lyricism, it threatens several times to go over the top, before being redeemed again by Steven's pleasingly sincere piano refrain. Released as a single in November 1975.

"ROCKS"

ROCKS

(ORIGINAL RELEASE: MAY 1976; CD RELEASE COLUMBIA/CBS 4749652)

Basking in the tremendous success of 'Toys In The Attic' and high as proverbial kites, Aerosmith began the difficult task of following up their breakthrough album by going to ground. Their newly accorded star status affording them the opportunity of a pre-production period, the group ensconced themselves in the cosy confines of the Wherehouse, in Waltham, Massachusetts, where fledgling riffs and chord progressions could be nurtured into the songs that would form 'Rocks'.

However, progress was slow. As usual, Steven was having trouble completing lyrics, and Joe Perry's recently forged alliance with heroin (a habit in which his partner Tyler was already skilled) meant many delays and false starts. Nevertheless, internal frustrations aside, when Aerosmith did finally run with the ball and transfer their efforts to the more luxurious surroundings of New York's Record Plant, it became clear they had a masterpiece on their hands.

With Jack Douglas again there to guide them, Aerosmith had appeared to distil their very spirit onto tape with 'Rocks', the nine tracks they produced for the album seeming to glitter with a dark majesty – flawless in execution and faultless in performance. As Aerosmith biographer Mark Putterford stated, 'If 'Toys In The Attic' defined Aerosmith's sound, then 'Rocks' perfected it.'

Simply put, each song was a rare gem. From the primal energy of 'Lick And A Promise' to the clipped funk of 'Last Child' the album literally pulsated. Yet it was more than that: Aerosmith had entered a new stage in their development here – with the sheets of sound and other-worldly dissonance that blessed the ending of 'Get The Lead Out' and the ungodly guitar drones that formed the backbone of 'Back In The Saddle', it was almost as if the group were nearer jazz in their improvisational quality, recalling the genius of Coltrane and Davis as much as Jagger and Richards.

Or perhaps, it was just the drugs. While the band were surely at the height of their creative powers, it has to be acknowledged that they were jacked to the nines while recording the LP, and ideas were as likely to be generated by snorts and tokes as pedals and effects. Narcotics would eventually dull Aerosmith's brilliance but not just yet.

Released in May 1976 in an ornate black cover featuring five sharply lit diamonds, there had initially been some trouble finding a name for the record. But when Tyler had questioned Perry as to the problem, the guitarist simply said, 'Call it 'Rocks''. Why? 'Because it does'. Dilemma solved, 'Rocks' shipped platinum (eventually selling more than 4 million copies) and cemented their status forever.

As dark as rum and swirling in deep, almost hallucinatory mists, its opaque

splendour has few equals in American hard rock, with only Van Halen's eponymous début album coming to mind as a possible contender.

Guns N' Roses' Slash sums up its unique appeal, 'I chased the most beautiful girl... for about three months. And when I finally got into her apartment, she played me 'Rocks' for the first time. I listened to it four or five times, completely forgot the girl, and split the apartment. That's what Aerosmith mean to me.'

'Rocks' then. A cure for sexual longing.

BACK IN THE SADDLE
(Tyler, Perry)

Cowboy Gothic. This Perry/Tyler penned homage to the old West sets the mood perfectly for all that's to follow. Beginning with doomy, climbing guitar chords, the song breaks wide open as it hits the chorus, transporting the listener instantaneously into the heart of Doc Holliday country.

Powered along by Perry's snaky six-string bass riff (its weary, grumbling tone pre-dating grunge by a good twelve years), and Kramer's inspired drumming, 'Back In The Saddle' documents clearly one of the group's principle strengths: the ability of the individual instruments to lock collectively into the beat, so freeing Steven Tyler to do his thing with the central melody. And what a job he does. Throat 100% open, the hyper-active frontman doesn't so much sing as howl the lyrics, turning the phrase 'riding high' alone into an awesome banshee wail.

'Back In The Saddle' would soon become Aerosmith's most reliable set opener – the position it would retain for years to come – as well as an inspiration to potential rock and roll gunslingers the world over. It certainly did the trick for a young Jon Bon Jovi, who seems to have built a career on the theme – 'I'm a cowboy, on a steel horse I ride'. Indeed.

LAST CHILD
(Tyler, Whitford)

A Whitford/Tyler composition this time, 'Last Child' is just about as funky as white boys are allowed to get. With the entire ensemble following a deceptively simple, rhythmic figure, Aerosmith catch the groove and ride it home for over three glorious minutes. Kramer comes into his own here, proving conclusively that all those nights spent playing with soul bands early in his musical career really did the trick. Tight and economical, and without the slightest hint of flash, his sticks simply dance.

The real treasure of the song though is not the killer instrumental performance, but the words that come with it. Tyler, his stream of consciousness psycho-babble now truly off the rails, offers us on 'Child' the best opportunity we'll ever get to enter the coked-out mind of this lyrical genius. If you thought 'Scuse Me While I Kiss The Sky' was deep, cop this: 'My hot-tail poontang sweetheart sweat, that makes a silk purse from J Paul Getty and his ear... with his face in a beer'.

God only knows what he was going on about, but it makes the most perfect sense at high volume!

RATS IN THE CELLAR
(Tyler, Perry)

A tale of urban decay and survival set on the mean streets of New York, 'Rats In The Cellar' is a violently paced rocker, and perfect descendant of 'Toys In The Attic'. Almost cinematic in construction with its police sirens and running snare drum, the number manages to invoke an atmosphere of inner-city paranoia, ably enhanced by Tyler's swooping harmonica fills and Perry's Whistling solo guitars. 'Throw me in the slam, catch me if you can,' snarls the singer, cannily adding to the tension.

Yet as things start to build towards a moody climax, a motif disturbingly reminiscent of Fleetwood Mac's 'Rattlesnake Shake' surfaces, rather convincingly proving once and for all classical composer Stravinsky's point that, 'Great composers don't borrow, they steal'. Aerosmith would cheekily admit years later that it was indeed nicked (eventually even going as far as including their live cover of the Mac original on the compilation 'Pandora's Box') but original or not, it works admirably within its context and enables the group to race towards the finishing line in suitably dramatic fashion, before letting Kramer brings matters thunderingly to a close.

COMBINATION
(Perry)

A walk in the shadows with Joe Perry. His first solo composition, based on a sluggish, almost slurred guitar riff, 'Combination' is a sullen and brooding animal, never quite at home with itself, and strangely all the better for it. Employing eerie, dreamlike lyrics and a discordant dual vocal attack, the song is a radical departure from the rest of 'Rocks', but seems somehow to define the inherent darkness pervading the album. It also effectively highlights the guitarist's skills on the fretboard, the solo alone being worth the price of admission.

Stepping in and out of the beat, Perry bends and twists, choosing odd notes and intervals to drive home the emotional point, before scaling the neck of his Strat at frightening speed to crash into the chorus, still intact. Slash would take the bones of this idea some ten years later for his own moment of glory on Guns N' Roses' 'Welcome To The Jungle' – albeit with less spectacular effect.

However, if 'Combination' has a sole claim to fame in Aerosmith's musical Cannon, it's down to the marvellous rhyming couplet, which though humorous now, is a timely reminder of their delicate hold on superstardom, wealth and the hazards that come with it: 'Walking on Gucci, wearing Yves St Laurent, barely stand up, cause I'm so goddamn gaunt.'

SICK AS A DOG
(Tyler, Hamilton)

Conversely, the brightest moment on the record, 'Sick As A Dog' is a pop-inflected singalong, a million miles away from its nauseous title. Written predominantly by bassist Tom Hamilton, it sees the white haired one switching to rhythm guitar for a change, allowing Perry and Tyler to experiment on four strings, and cover his day job. Pleasing guitar harmonies (unusual for Aerosmith) and the use of hand claps to accentuate that chorus made the song extremely radio friendly, and a live fan favourite to boot.

NOBODY'S FAULT
(Tyler, Whitford)

With music provided by Whitford – 'One of a long string of Brad Whitford songs in key of F-sharp,' quipped Hamilton – and Tyler's lyrics dwelling on the dangers of an earthquake along California's San Andreas fault, Aerosmith get off the leash for this one. A deceptive church organ announcing its introduction (actually, volume swells courtesy of the guitars) the track soon roars into life, forsaking all subtleties in its quest for blood. With a fine vocal take from Steven, inspired time keeping from Kramer and his kick-drum, and Mr Whitford simply incendiary on

several wah-wah solos, 'Nobody's Fault' is not for the faint hearted.

GET THE LEAD OUT
(Tyler, Perry)

Pointing two fingers at the Studio 54 disco craze prevalent at the time, Tyler and Perry's hymn to the alternative dance floor sees the band return from the previous track's violence, into a more groove orientated feel. Recalling Led Zeppelin with its swinging, tight but loose guitars and lurching back beat, 'Get The Lead Out' is still wholly Aerosmith's own thing – replete with that trademark 'fizz'.

Nevertheless, it's the fade out that really draws one's attention, with waves of dissonance and feedback merging trance-like into Tyler's half-spoken vocals and Perry's cut glass slide work.

LICK AND A PROMISE
(Tyler, Perry)

Truly touched by the hand of God and loud as a pneumatic drill, 'Lick And A

Promise' is Aerosmith's greatest recorded moment. Lurching into life with a psychotic ascending scale – which pulls the neat trick of completely disorientating the audience before the fun begins in earnest – we're slapped back into reality with Tyler's opening gambit: 'Johnny come lately on a Saturday night.' From here on in it's rock and roll heaven. Marvellous lyrical imagery, steeped in ragged decadence, a career-best performance from the engine room of Joey Kramer and Tom Hamilton, and frying valves, warped fretboards and country-like runs from Perry and Whitford ensure that if the group had died after nailing this one, their legend would be for all time secure.

HOME TONIGHT
(Tyler)

A wistful, Tyler-penned ballad with a 101 piece orchestra enlisted to add some extra class, 'Home Tonight' does the job of closing 'Rocks' in fine style. Reminiscent of 'You See Me Crying' from 'Toys In The Attic' and featuring unusual harmony vocals from Kramer, a restrained tuneful solo from Perry and a grand turn at the piano from the frontman, our heartstrings are tugged, our tear ducts activated and we're left wanting more.

DRAW THE LINE

(ORIGINAL RELEASE: DECEMBER 1977; CD RELEASE COLUMBIA/CBS 4749662)

'We saw it as a sort of vacation. So we went off and rented a nunnery and it was just total party time.' – Joe Perry on 'Draw The Line'.

Though American dates for the promotion of 'Rocks' had gone well, Aerosmith's eagerly awaited European jaunt had largely died on its feet. Arriving like visiting royalty in the midst of the punk explosion, and greeted with hostility from critics and casual indifference from festival crowds for their newly acquired royal behaviour, the band returned to US shores smarting from the jibes, and with another album to make – not the best combination.

Nevertheless, there was still enough unbowed arrogance and ego-boosting cocaine left in Aerosmith to feel confident that they still had the goods to slay unbelievers. And so, guitars in hand, they descended on Armonk, New York State, with a mobile recording desk and enough pharmaceuticals to equip a hospital, to record the follow up, their next *magnum opus*.

Their destination was The Cenacle. A huge, disused nunnery with spacious rooms and natural reverb, it seemed the perfect venue for the quintet and their entourage to unwind from the recent rigours of touring, and get those creative juices flowing once again. However, to say what happened next recalled the last days of The Roman Empire would only be gross understatement.

Rumours abound about Aerosmith's recording of 'Draw The Line' – there's the one about Joe Perry losing the original demos the band had written for the album one drunken night, only to have his wife find them days later in a biscuit tin. Another about various members leaving the group out of frustration in the middle of recording, only to be talked round with huge offers of money by frantic management. Endless delays, crippling hangovers, automobile accidents and copious ingestion of cocaine to fuel the inspirational fires constitute a further four. But perhaps the best centres around a guitar player who, bored beyond belief by his partner's inability to complete the lyrics, took to shooting at random targets from the rooftops of the make-shift studio, cursing loudly with each miss.

Whether true or not one thing was certain, Aerosmith were fully paid up members of The Twilight Zone during the making of the album and the music was coming a poor second place to the party. Their general mood was summed up well in an interview with Rolling Stone in 1990. 'We'd gotten to that dangerous point where we could afford all our vices.'

That said, though recording was painfully slow and motivation clear as fog, there were eventually to be flashes of genius on the record. The super-charged title track, brimmng with venom and energy is one such, and the drunken

blues swagger of 'Can't Get It Up' another, but the pinpoint focus of 'Rocks' was gone, replaced in part by uneven jamming and studio gimmicks.

Aerosmith and Jack Douglas (still manning the helm) would finally leave the padded walls of The Cenacle to tidy things up at LA's Record Plant, fusing the contributions of guest musicians such as pianist Scott Cushnie and saxophonist Stan Bronstein to the tracks, just in time for a December 1977 release. Dispensing with the services of Pacific Eye and Ear, who had designed the covers for 'Toys In The Attic' and 'Rocks' in favour of cartoon legend Al Hirschfeld, 'Draw The Line' carried a merciless caricature of the band into many a teenager's Christmas stocking that year.

In spite of the torturous atmosphere surrounding its creation, the record, like its predecessors, was immediately accorded platinum status and another round of touring was booked to support further sales. However, while ticket sales climbed, the critics sounded caution, with Crawdaddy's Toby Goldstein expressing the majority's opinion: 'The band shows a deadly wear and tear on their creativity.' And their central nervous systems, by the sound of it...

On a personal note, I, like many Aerosmith fans, have a soft spot for the LP, enjoying its clattering soundtrack of car crashes, inflamed sinuses and empty Bourbon bottles. Yet I have to concede, discipline is not being exercised here.

DRAW THE LINE
(Tyler, Perry)
Roaring out of the starting gates, Aerosmith choose to open their fifth studio album with a reckless abandon that leaves the listener gasping for breath. With its screaming vocals, white-knuckle slide guitars and padded-cell drumming, this Tyler/Perry penned ode to God knows what really shakes and moves. Throw in a grizzly, industrial mid-track breakdown, and a frontman definitely in need of sedatives by the song's end, 'Draw The Line' is the nearest thing the Seventies got to speed-metal. And I

didn't mention amphetamines once.

I WANNA KNOW WHY
(Tyler, Perry)
Keeping up the pace, Aerosmith turn to the Stones for musical inspiration and provide a bluesy meltdown of a song that would sit quite nicely on 'Exile On Main Street'. Covered in brass and bouncing along on the back of a jaunty, ragtime piano courtesy of Scott Cushnie, Tyler gets pissed off with 'Everybody's Good Intentions', before letting Brad Whitford torture the neck of his Gibson Les Paul.

CRITICAL MASS
(Tyler, Hamilton, Douglas)
Stumble number one. Though immaculately produced by Jack Douglas, whose experimental flourishes with the sound keep things reasonably interesting, this dislocated collection of ideas looking for a home never quite gel, and leave the track lost at sea. Only Scott Cushnie's spirited piano-break and Tyler's discordant

harmonica fills find the life raft, but it's not enough.

However, the number remains a firm favourite with the band, turning up on the hand-picked compilation 'Gems'.

CAN'T GET IT UP
(Tyler, Perry)

A chaotic mess, but still marvellous. Joe Perry once said that Aerosmith's sound could be described as, 'Hanging by a thread', and this track is the proof. Constructed around a drunken, half-asleep slide lick from the guitarist, and featuring a meandering nonsensical lyric from Tyler (bemoaning his inability to rise

to the occasion). You can actually see the beer bottles piling up in the corner as the band try and get the groove. Rhythms clash, pianos bump into basses, and yet somehow it all comes right in the end. Lord knows what Karen Lawrence (drafted in for some sore throat backing vocals) made of it at the time though.

BRIGHT LIGHT FRIGHT
(Perry)

Or Perry goes punk. Written by the moody one in a fit of pique, this howling protest to daylight hours is an out of control pile-up, chock full of tortured Strats and shrieking saxophones. Sung by Joe himself, with lines such as 'It's the dawn of the day and I'm crashed and I'm smashed, as it is I'm feeling like my chips are cashed', it paints a vampire-like picture of life on the road.

An intolerant 'screw the world' stomper, it was great to see the band take it out of mothballs for their appearance at Donington in 1994, though hopes for a regular spot in the set remain somewhat unrealistic.

KINGS AND QUEENS
(Hamilton, Kramer, Tyler, Whitford, Douglas)

Rousing, if somewhat ponderous, 'Kings And Queens' sees Aerosmith enter epic territory. A band effort with producer Jack Douglas and Paul Prestopino adding atmospheric mandolin and banjo to the pot, this mediaeval tale of Vikings and holy wars and blood-soaked Englishmen has its moments – those jagged 'psycho'-like violin squeals on the main riff come especially to mind – but it does tend to outstay its welcome towards the end.

Still, there's some fine solo work from Tom Hamilton and Brad Whitford to reflect on, and Joey Kramer sounds like he's having a ball with the numerous tempo upheavals.

THE HAND THAT FEEDS
(Hamilton, Kramer, Tyler, Whitford, Douglas)

Despite some jazzy chord changes and an impressive performance from the engine room of Hamilton and Kramer, this boogie by numbers can't escape its rather ordinary status. Even Tyler sounds as if he'd rather be elsewhere. With the amount of drugs that went into the LP, he probably was.

SIGHT FOR SORE EYES
(Tyler, Perry)

Much better. Sassy, gin-soaked and with Tyler back in fine insidious form, Aerosmith really get to grips with this funk-rock shuffle. Recalling previous gems such as 'Walk This Way' and

'GetThe Lead Out', the group work up a real head of steam, pummelling the song's riff every which way before letting Perry loose to close proceedings with some tremolo heavy solo guitar.

MILK COW BLUES
(Arnold)

A slow burning moody treatment of the 1934 Kokomo Arnold standard, 'Milk Cow Blues' three note hook certainly brings the album to a close likeably enough. However, its inclusion remains mystifying. Did the band really need to plunder its formative live set for material and if so, why wheel out this old chestnut? Brad Whitford has told rock magazine *Trouser Press* that he still listens to the old 'Draw The Line' demos in his car, adding, 'There are some incredible tracks that never got on the record.' It seems a pity then that we get a cover version (albeit a 'goodun') when there may have been so many other hidden treasures worthy of release.

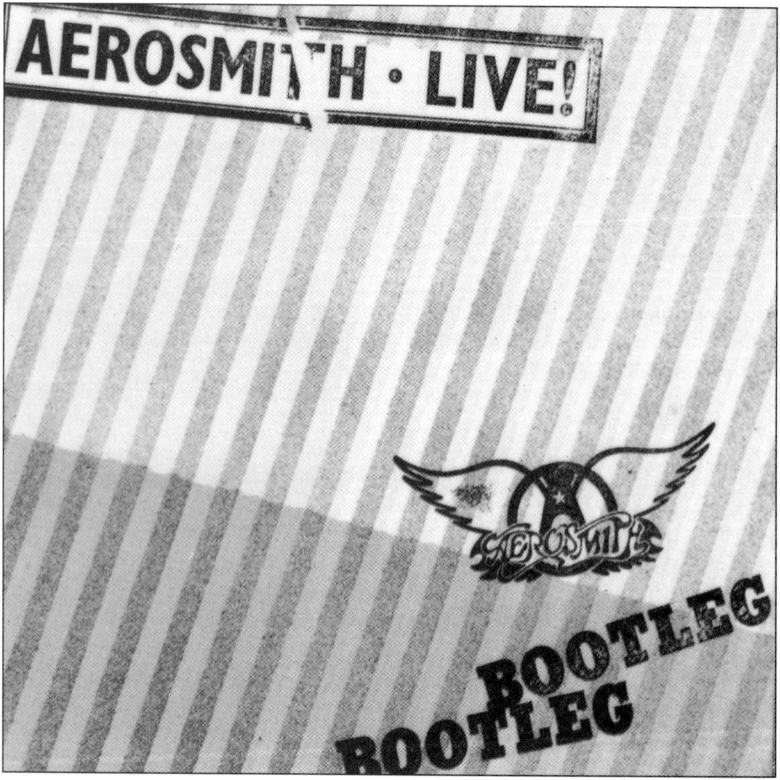
AEROSMITH · LIVE!
AEROSMITH
BOOTLEG
BOOTLEG

LIVE! BOOTLEG

(ORIGINAL RELEASE: NOVEMBER 1978; CD RELEASE COLUMBIA/CBS 4749672)

With the benefit of hindsight, Aerosmith's 'Live! Bootleg' is a raw and exciting record, illustrating effectively a coked-out rock monster at the heights of its powers – good and bad. Yet at the time of its release, its cripplingly honest approach must have proved an earache to many FM radio programmers who had grown used to lulling their listeners into easy submission with the anodyne pleasures of Peter Frampton's 'Comes Alive'.

Blunt, direct and with little after-the-event studio enhancement so beloved of official concert sets, 'Bootleg''s main weapon is that it sounds so real. Notes are fluffed, vocal lines shy well away from those high notes, and on occasion the band descend into a musical abyss, instruments clashing with each other, before jarring uneasily to a close. Yet it is this spontaneity of approach that makes it such compelling listening. And as a document of Aerosmith live *circa* 1973-1978, it more than serves its purpose.

At the time of issue, Aerosmith were still sporadically on the road in support of their previous effort, 'Draw The Line', though it would be true to say that by then their chemical voyages were creating some real problems. Unpredictable sets (Tyler being carried on stage more often than not in a junked up stupor, before the adrenaline kicked in to carry him through the gig), fraying tempers and other general signs of burn-out were becoming the norm, and it was clear to both group and management that another studio record would not be on the cards for some time. A stop-gap was needed and 'Bootleg' was it.

Hastily assembling a collection of performances drawn predominantly from recent sets, the band, with the assistance of then sixth member Jack Douglas, set about making minimal repairs – "Anybody who tells you they didn't fix anything on a live album is strictly inaccurate, said Joe Perry – before releasing it to an eager market, already primed by their recent concert experiences. Suffice to say, the trick worked, and the LP shipped the now *de rigueur* platinum.

'Live! Bootleg' also had the effect of giving Aerosmith back some of the monetary action that had been lost to unofficial live recordings of their sound. 'I was getting ticked off at seeing lots of bootlegs... it was time to jump on it,' said Tyler at the time, though with its misshapen cardboard cover, replete with coffee stains and uneven rubber stamps declaring 'Bootleg' all over it, it was sometimes difficult to distinguish from other black market Aerosmith product.

Stop-gap or middle finger to opportunists it matters not, 'Bootleg' remains Aerosmith's only live album to date (Kiss had by now managed four!), and while it's not on a par with 'The Who Live At Leeds' or Thin Lizzy's ground-breaking 'Live And Dangerous', it retains enough magic and undiluted power to see off many other 'live' pretenders. At its purest, 'Live! Bootleg' is rock and roll with the chemicals left in.

Edited highlights and previously unreleased material are detailed below:

SWEET EMOTION/LORD OF THE THIGHS

Chance taking, extended performances of both songs are featured here from a '78 Chicago show, with the group teetering dangerously out of control at times, and all the better for it. Drummer Joey Kramer bravely holds the fort as guitars shriek and hiss (Whitford providing an astonishing lead break on 'Sweet Emotion') and Tyler adds a marvellously malevolent vocal to 'Lord Of The Thighs', considerably increasing the tension present in the song's strange lyrics.

TOYS IN THE ATTIC

Taken from a triumphant homecoming gig in Boston, March 1978, 'Toys' here bears little resemblance to the tight and

punctuated version that graces the quintet's landmark third album. It's more a case of 'no brakes, more fun' as the song pummels along at uncontrollable speed. Hamilton's instrumental prowess nevertheless remains undiminished, as he still manages to nail the track's complex mid section bass fills with disarming ease.

Point of interest: what exactly is it that Joe Perry says off-mike at 2 minutes 34 seconds into the track? And more to the point, who's he saying it to?

COME TOGETHER

Lifted from a live rehearsal at the Wherehouse, Waltham, Massachusetts, where according to the band, 'We kept the gig so secret, nobody showed up but us', Aerosmith turn in an inspirational cover of the Lennon/McCartney tune, dripping with bluesy piano (courtesy of Aerosmith's touring keyboardist of the time, Mark Radice), and lazy, behind-the-beat guitars. This version slays the studio cut, recorded for Aerosmith's appearance in the appalling *Sgt Pepper's Lonely*

Hearts Club Band movie. Nice handclaps at the end as well.

WALK THIS WAY

For many, the definitive take. Rousing, amiable and greatly benefiting from a shot of concert adrenaline (being provided here by an appreciative 1978 Detroit crowd) the whole band give it all they've got to produce a Mardi Gras treatment of this classic song. Hats off, particularly to Joey Kramer for some brisk stickwork and Joe Perry for those staggering voice box-effected guitars.

CHIP AWAY THE STONE

Previously unreleased on album at the time, this Richie Supa penned Rolling Stones homage is awash with chunky guitars and swirling synthesisers. The version here, recorded at Santa Monica's Civic Auditorium in 1978, gives some indication as to why Aerosmith thought it could be a potential hit single, but as fans never accorded it the same respect, it was soon dropped.

I AIN'T GOT YOU/MOTHER POPCORN

Liberated from a stereo simulcast recorded by Boston's WCBN radio station in April 1973, these early examples of the Aerosmith sound give a clear indication of the band's formative influences – namely The Yardbirds and James Brown. Even though the sound quality is a little flaky, their inclusion alone on 'Live! Bootleg' is much appreciated. Funky, measured and brimming with youthful intent, Aerosmith sound relaxed and confident, clearly a group on the rise. Tyler is undoubtedly the star, giving a heart-stopping vocal on 'Popcorn' that would have you believe his range to be limitless. Smoky sax from David Woodford provides the proverbial cherry on the top.

TRAIN KEPT A ROLLIN'

Loose limbed and outpacing most thrash metal, Aerosmith burn down Detroit in February 1976, with this, their theme tune. Tyler howls, Perry doffs his cap to Hendrix with a showy intersong rendition

of Sinatra's 'Strangers In The Night' and the firecrackers... crack. As encores go, it's rather good.

Other tracks available on 'Live! Bootleg' – 'Back In The Saddle', 'Last Child', 'Sick As A Dog', 'Dream On', 'Sight For Sore Eyes', 'Mama Kin/ S.O.S.', 'Draw The Line' (bonus track unlisted on sleeve).

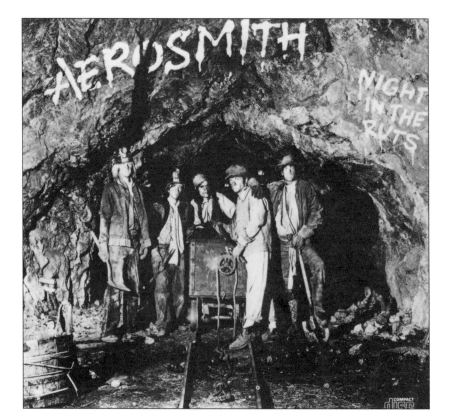

NIGHT IN THE RUTS

(ORIGINAL RELEASE: NOVEMBER 1979; CD RELEASE COLUMBIA/CBS 4749682)

The cover says it all really. Five grim faced young men staring bleakly into a camera from the confines of a black pit. The party was over.

By 1979 years of incessant touring, copious drug use and increasingly frail egos had stretched marital relations between Steven Tyler and Joe Perry to breaking point. The dynamic duo, whose writing partnership had unleashed the best moments found on 'Toys In The Attic', 'Rocks' and 'Draw The Line' were now barely communicating, and the strain it was putting on the band was intolerable. With Perry in debt to the band/management for the sum of $100,000 (and having to provide a solo album to clean the slate), it was only a matter of time before something broke.

Returning to the Wherehouse in Waltham for pre-production duties before transferring to Manhattan's Mediasound Studio to begin recording proper, Aerosmith's management company, Leber-Krebs, installed a new engineer/producer to oversee the group, having somewhat ungraciously dispensed with the services of regular producer Jack Douglas early in proceedings. Gary Lyons, whose previous credits included work with Foreigner and Humble Pie, was chosen primarily as a cost cutting exercise, his abilities to both record and produce the quintet seen as a way of reducing overheads – and for the group, freeing up drug money. Unfortunately, the ruse didn't work.

The hostility between Tyler and Perry, then at fever-pitch, meant that the singer and guitarist would not even enter the studios at the same time. So, according to Lyons, 'Joe came in first and got all his guitar parts done', leaving Steven the task of completing lyrics and melodies to

the tunes they had written. However, the frontman, in the throes of opium addiction, was hardly in a fit state to walk – let alone sing. Thousands of dollars in recording time were frittered away as a result. The only option left to Aerosmith to recoup their losses was to suspend recording and go back on tour.

Tired, wasted and hauling across North America against their will, it wasn't long before in-fighting again broke out and Perry, stretched beyond all

endurance, walked. 'I washed my hands of it,' he said at the time. The tour in tatters, it was left to the remaining members to return to New York and complete the album, calling on guest guitarists Richie Supa, Neil Thompson and new member-in-waiting, Jimmy Crespo, to fill any gaps. Months later (and at a suspected cost of over one million dollars), 'Night In The Ruts' was eventually released.

Despite the débâcle that surrounded its recording (now a re-current theme), the LP itself was pretty good. Riff-heavy and with a crisp, no-nonsense sound. 'Ruts' walked a fine line between *Led Zeppelin* and the Stones, but with enough individuality present to refute 'copyist' cries. However, with three cover tunes present, original material did not seem to have been a primary concern. As usual, it sold – but not in the same numbers as usual. Aerosmith were in trouble...

Joe Perry, who through his superlative guitar work really owns 'Right In The Nuts' (as it was affectionately known) still rates the album, telling *Rock Scene* magazine: 'I think a really good representation of what Aerosmith does is on 'Night In The Ruts' – that's really an underrated record.' Nevertheless, it will still mainly be remembered by fans as the LP that broke the band.

NO SURPRIZE
(Tyler, Perry)

'Night In The Ruts' starts with a bang, courtesy of this no-nonsense, Stones-inflected boogie. An auto-biographical account of the band's hard fought battle to stardom helped along by Gary Lyon's spare 'record what's there' production and the edgy, abrasive guitars (Richie Supa helping out on rhythm for the absent Perry), Tyler takes the helm here, weaving a tale of humble beginnings to full blown fame through the verses, before exploding in a humorous lyrical finger-pointing exercise at the record company that's come to rule him at the track's end: 'If Japanese can boil teas, then where the fuck's my royalties?'

Brisk, emotive and superbly performed, it remains one of Aerosmith's most simple and effective rockers – a proud first cousin to the likes of 'Mama Kin' and 'No More, No More'.

CHIQUITA
(Tyler, Perry)

Aerosmith keep up the pressure with this massively powerful slab of hard rock dynamics. Featuring enough classic Perry riffs to sink a battleship and a stop/start rhythm pattern that lurches

menacingly ever forward, 'Chiquita' is all twists and turns, Tyler inventing melody after melody just to keep up. Add an insistent, stabbing brass section (courtesy of George Young, Lou Delgotto, Lou Marini and Barry Rogers) and it's up there with the best of them.

REMEMBER (WALKING IN THE SAND)
(Morton)

Oh dear. Tyler's tribute to soul music divas The Shangri-La's, ('The Shangri-La's were always one of my all time favourite groups,' he told *Creem* journalist Annene Kaye) proves a tired and lumpy affair, never once capturing the original track's romantic, ethereal quality. Replete with cod-finger snaps and a half asleep bassline from Hamilton, you're glad when the ending arrives.

CHEESE CAKE
(Tyler, Perry)

'And on the eighth day God created Joe Perry.'

Despite exiting Aerosmith mid-way through the recording of 'Night In The Ruts' what Perry did leave behind is nothing short of astonishing – and 'Cheese Cake' is the best evidence of it. Evolving from his bluesy, swaggering riff, this lusty ode to another of Tyler's women sees the guitarist switching from lap steel to six-string and back in one take, and proving master of both. Emotive, authoritative and fully in synch with the groove, Joe's playing here is simply a revelation.

However, he's not surrounded by slouches. As the song moves through light and shade, dropping and picking up the tempo to emphasise Tyler's lyrics, Hamilton (now fully awake) and Kramer react in perfect concert, accenting those all-important lulls with economy and occasionally silence. Whoever said you're only as good as your rhythm section wasn't joking!. A great song, cut mostly live, it's 'Ruts'' highpoint.

THREE MILE SMILE
(Tyler, Perry)

Another corker, concentrating on Aerosmith's more funky traits this time. Using that famous push/pull technique of theirs, 'Three Mile Smile' is reminiscent of Led Zeppelin's 'Out On The Tiles' in construction, bouncing the two main hooks present off each other to create that all-important tension. Blessed with a cheeky, almost nervous vocal from Tyler and yet another star performance from Joey Kramer, if Aerosmith were suffering at this time from drug overload and AWOL guitarists, this track certainly doesn't show it.

Rumours persist that Joe Perry's eventual replacement, Jimmy Crespo, provides the solo guitars present on 'Three Mile Smile'. However, he is not credited on the LP's liner notes.

REEFER HEAD WOMAN
(Melrose, Bennett, Gillum)

Cover number two, this time of the 1945 Melrose, Bennett and Gillum blues tune.

Slow, swaying and packed with drug references – 'I got a reefer head woman, she fell right down from the sky' – the band relax you into this track before temporarily turning up the heat in the middle. Authentic Delta vocals and harmonica from Tyler, and a meltdown solo from Perry give the song a silver star, but the lack of original material is again springing to mind.

BONE TO BONE (CONEY ISLAND WHITE FISH BOY)
(Tyler, Perry)

Or 'Condom', to those of us living outside New York City State. A rubbery, frenetic assault course of a song, charging around its cascading main riff with great speed. Tyler gets hot under the collar with a cock-sure story of a wild beach boy looking for love, while Perry and Whitford embark on a guitar war using wah pedals and distortion units as their aural ammunition. Piping hot, and unrestrained .

THINK ABOUT IT
(Relf, McCarty, Page)

Cover number three. This time Aerosmith warm up The Yardbirds' philosophical classic and in doing so, pay another debt to their main source of inspiration. Taken at speed (or with it) but kept tight as tuppence by Kramer's metronome-like snare, they stay reasonably faithful to the McCarty/Relf/Page original until the track's middle section when all hell breaks loose. Joe Perry, seemingly intent on staking his claim as America's answer to Jeff Beck, simply explodes. Howling feedback, tremolo bar dive bombs, chicken-like fretboard scratches, mental string bends, they're all on display from the formidable Perry arsenal. He once said, 'There's nothing like a tortured Strat' – and he's right, creating sheer pandemonium here.

Suffice to say, restoring musical equilibrium after this insanely gifted lead break is impossible, but Tyler does his best, invoking his own angry demons in an inspired vocal take to get the band home in one piece. Absent or otherwise, 'Think About It''s guitar wizardry conclusively proved that 'Night In The Ruts' was Perry's album, and a two fingered salute to anyone who thought Aerosmith would not miss his fire.

MIA
(Tyler)

Written to celebrate the birth of Tyler's baby girl – the song's title bears her name – 'Mia' is a surprisingly dark ballad, swirling around a lonesome piano refrain beautifully played by Steven. More Grimm's Fairy Tale than Walt Disney, the song slows to a halt with a single repeated keyboard note, its low and ominous tone sounding like a malevolent grandfather clock. Ghostly and evocative, 'Mia' is a troubled father's love song to his child.

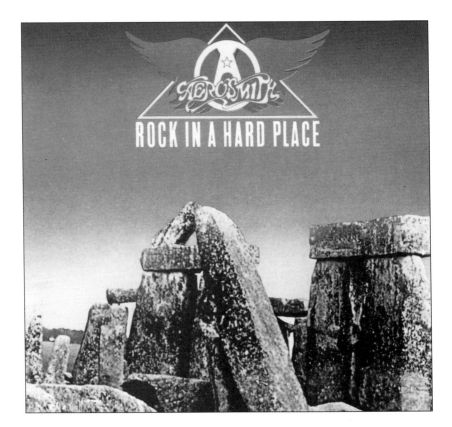

ROCK IN A HARD PLACE

(ORIGINAL RELEASE: AUGUST 1982; CD RELEASE COLUMBIA/CBS 4749702)

Aerosmith were to audition many guitarists in their search to replace Joe Perry, UFO's Michael Schenker and Rick Derringer's Danny Johnson being just two of the more notable applicants. However, their quest would come to an end after meeting the unassuming yet quietly confident Jimmy Crespo. Crespo, a native New Yorker who had paid his dues with RCA rock hopefuls Flame, was not only an accomplished player and ideas man, but also bore more than a passing resemblance to Aerosmith's previous axe-slinger – a good sign in Tyler's eyes. Several rehearsals and a few beers later, he was in.

Nevertheless, it would be nearly two years before he would see his official recorded début with the band released. The reason – Steven Tyler. With Aerosmith's financial fortunes ever declining and reduced to feeding his now out of control drug habit from the sleazy environs of a Manhattan hotel, the vocalist was topping the list of the 'next dead celebrity' contest. When Tyler lost his heel in a motorcycle accident and was sent to bed for much of 1980, it seemed certain that it was all over for the quintet. Surprisingly, they carried on.

Preparing new material at The Wherehouse in Boston (and posting tapes to the frontman for opinions), Aerosmith bravely soldiered forward through the year, with Crespo providing many of the song ideas. Yet, the still frequent bouts of inactivity and Tyler's precarious health proved too much for Brad Whitford, who finally threw in his towel in 1981, when still no new Aero-product had been produced.

Replaced by colourful unknown Rick Dufay (whose Keith Richards-like persona suited the group well), and with Tyler again sufficiently well to re-join the ranks, Aerosmith would eventually get it

together in early 1982, venturing to Miami, Florida to start work in earnest on the follow up to 'Night In The Ruts'.

Having initially begun the album with producer Tony Bongiovi – yes, second cousin to Jon – Aerosmith found the formative results too 'new wave' for their liking, and so cap in hand, they returned to old friend Jack Douglas to tidy up the mess. Douglas, ever the catalyst, seemed to make the critical difference as

the record finally came together in fits and starts by the summer of 1982.

The personnel pile-up that had gone into making what would be christened 'Rock in A Hard Place' was extraordinary. Pieced together at Miami's Criteria Studios with touch-ups added at New York's Power Station, the group had lost one guitarist, gained two, used eleven supplementary musicians, seven assistant engineers and two producers. Surely the LP was at best going to be patchy?

As if to spite detractors, 'Rock in A Hard Place' turned out an unexpected pleasure. Giving away little of the uphill struggle it had been to complete, it saw Aerosmith nicely into the Eighties, their sound toughening up to the challenge of a new decade, and disposing any young pretenders who had sought their throne in the band's absence. Tracks such as 'Jailbait' and 'Bolivian Ragamuffin' coursed with energy and Tyler's lyrical humour – always a major weapon – was retained on cuts like 'Bitches Brew' and 'Push Comes To Shove'. Though certainly no masterpiece, it was a striking

return and a major feather in Jimmy Crespo's hat, having proved himself up to the gargantuan task of breathing new life into Aerosmith's old bones.

The sleeve though was a different story. Featuring Spinal Tap-like standing stones against a lurid blue background, it caused many guffaws amongst fans and certainly didn't aid the record's sales. 'I took Spinal Tap real personal,' was Steven's measured response at the time.

At a cost of nearly 1.5 million dollars and the near break-up of the group, 'Rock in A Hard Place' still remains at the time of writing, the only Aerosmith LP not accorded platinum status. Nonetheless, it served the critical purpose of holding the fort a little longer, until Tyler and Perry finally put those old wounds to rest, and got on with the show.

JAILBAIT
(Tyler, Crespo)

Eager to keep up the tradition of opening their albums with a bang, Aerosmith don't disappoint here. A lyrical walk through the fields of under-age lust, taken at mach-speed, 'Jailbait' is all abrasive vocals, surging volume swells and thunderous drumming. Replacement Jimmy Crespo makes his presence felt immediately - more textural than Perry, his distorted landscape of guitars engulf the sound, pushing it further towards heavy metal perhaps, but without falling prey to the histrionics that sometimes accompany that genre.

'Jailbait' remains Tyler's show though, with a grandstand performance from the frontman. Oblivious to the chaos around him, he epitomises lascivious intent, rolling the song's all too obvious title around his mouth before spitting it out in a hundred different variations before the end comes. Still Aerosmith then, but with a harder edge.

LIGHTNING STRIKES
(Supa)

Rising ominously from the speakers, a church-like organ announces the arrival of this Richie Supa penned street-gang anthem. With edgy guitars and goose-step drumming soon fading in to join those keys, it's almost a relief when Tyler bursts out of the speakers with his ratty call to arms – 'Boys in the street are ready to rumble...'

Essentially a Stones-like shuffle, Douglas' canny production turns this track into a mini-epic. Never losing the band's cantankerous vibe, he adds and subtracts from the rhythm, establishing pace and tension, and thus completely grabbing the listener's attention.

It would come to light years later that Perry was as sick as a proverbial dog not to have played on 'Lightning Strikes', and more than a little jealous of how well they had done without him!

BITCHES BREW
(Tyler, Crespo)

A sulphurous, mean-spirited rocker, lyrically all seething cauldrons, brimstone and broomsticks. Featuring great turns from Tyler and Crespo (who really seemed to be getting the hang of this Aerosmith lark) the song's highlight comes in the middle section when the band get the funk out in vintage style.

BOLIVIAN RAGAMUFFIN
(Tyler, Crespo)

White knuckles. This thinly disguised tribute to the cocaine trail is a brutal affair – overflowing with dislocated riffing and scatter-shot vocals. Written by Tyler and Crespo (who is responsible for six of the tracks on 'Rock in A Hard Place'), song structure is abandoned in favour of all-out attack, and at times 'Ragamuffin' suffers as a result. Nevertheless, as an exercise in shit-kicking musical violence it's just fine.

CRY ME A RIVER
(Hamilton)

Steven Tyler – 'I heard it in Beaumont, Texas... I had this old honky tonk station on, and they happened to play the oldie by Julie London, and I thought to myself it would be terrific to bring it back.' And rape it.

A gentle jazzy guitar and sweet, hesitant vocal introduce this cover of the old Julie London tear-jerker, lulling the listener into a dream-like sense of security. But within a minute or so, the solos start to whistle, the bass starts to pound, and Tyler's back to his old 'howling at the moon' self. Given a lighter treatment the song would have made a fine single but as it's presented here, it's another excuse to rock out. Pity.

PRELUDE TO JOANIE/ JOANIE'S BUTTERFLY
(Tyler) (Tyler, Crespo, Douglas)

A combination of a riff Jimmy Crespo came up with one lonely night in his hotel

room and a particularly vivid dream Steven Tyler had experienced, Jack Douglas joins Aerosmith's new writing team to produce this song in three parts.

Part one – 'Prelude to Joanie' – is a psychedelic freak-out recalling the singer's nocturnal vision of a pony sprouting wings. All distorted vocoder and Arabic chants, it's either very deep and meaningful or pretentious twaddle depending on your point of view.

Part two consolidates the story over a folky, acoustic guitar interlude. Recalling Led Zeppelin's more experimental moments with its shifting, clever chord work and backwards vocals, it's the strongest section of the track.

Part three is when the band joins in, and things hot up. Essentially standard Aerosmith fare, Richard Straub's violins and some truly odd percussion courtesy of Kramer and producer Douglas do help retain some of that earlier weirdness, but it still feels like Chuck Berry tackling 'Kashmir'.

Taken as an experiment, 'Joanie's Butterfly' isn't bad, if a little ambitious, and as guitarist Colin Stewart said – 'You can certainly hear the drugs in it!'

ROCK IN A HARD PLACE (CHESHIRE CAT)
(Tyler, Crespo)

The album's title track, and a real melting pot of jazz, blues and heavy metal. Warming up with Kramer's busy shuffle-beat and Tyler's snarling harmonica, Aerosmith soon take hold of the song's meaty hook and beat it to a pulp. Crespo shines, piling on layer upon layer of valve-soaked guitar, and Steven's impression of a Cheshire cat on heat has to be heard to be believed.

JIG IS UP
(Tyler, Crespo)

More flirting with jazz, though this time it's more fusion than New Orleans. Danceable, witty, and featuring a 'surely that's Joe Perry?' solo from Jimmy Crespo the track is certainly likeable enough, but it doesn't quite rise above being a collection of riffs, rather than a complete song. God bless Tim Hamilton though, whose crisp, twisting bass lines do their best to connect those missing dots...

PUSH COMES TO SHOVE
(Tyler)

The result of a mammoth 54-hour record-ing session engineered by Godfrey Diamond, 'Push Comes To Shove' sees Tyler as jack-of-all-trades and master of most. Turning his talents to harmonica, drums, piano and lead and backing vocals, he creates an inspired bar-room brawl of a ballad, mourning loves lost and beers downed. Wasted, strained and downright incomprehensible at times, according to Steven , 'It used to sound like a Burt Bacharach thing.' Perhaps it did, but here it's a companion piece to Tom Waits' 'The Piano Has Been Drinking'. Gloriously intoxicated.

THE GEFFEN YEARS
DONE WITH MIRRORS

(ORIGINAL RELEASE: NOVEMBER 1985; CD RELEASE GEFFEN 9240912)

Aerosmith MkII would last only another 18 months after the release of 'Rock In A Hard Place'. Still soaked in pharmaceuticals, their tour to support the album was either a glorious triumph or an embarrassing mess, depending on how in control they were on a given night. 'We did some great gigs and we did some awful gigs depending on how screwed up we were, especially Steven,' was guitarist Rick Dufay's telling comment.

Yet, however you cut it, the general consensus was that it just wasn't the same. To the band members the problem was obvious – Steven Tyler missed his twin. 'We just couldn't get Steven going,' admitted Jimmy Crespo. 'He wanted Perry back. It'd be like, 'Joe did this, Joe did that' [and] eventually I accepted that the only way Aerosmith would work well again would be if Joe and Brad returned.'

And so in the Spring of 1984 behind the scenes machinations began to re-unite the original line-up. Perry was sceptical at first, having just secured a gig with Alice Cooper and ever mindful of his former cohort's precarious state. Yet, similarly missing the glory days, and tempted by the cash a reunion could generate (Perry was as broke as Tyler following declining solo album sales and a messy divorce settlement) he finally acceded. It was just days before Whitford followed suit.

Nevertheless, there was still a legal minefield to negotiate before Aerosmith could get back in the saddle. Perry, now with new manager Tim Collins, was at the time suing the group's previous caretakers Leber-Krebs for neglect of commitment and refused point blank to work with them again. Therefore, the only choice left open to the newly re-formed quintet was to cut ties with Leber-Krebs and come under the control of Collins. It

wasn't long before they did the same with their label, Columbia, to whom they were still tied. Though Columbia initially put up a fight, they must have been secretly relieved at heart, having watched the dwindling royalties they paid Aerosmith go straight into the hands of drug dealers.

With no label, swamped in lawsuits and under new management, there was only one thing to do – hit the road. Repeating the logic of their Seventies heyday, 'Play and you get the people behind you', Aerosmith toured their arses off, completing 70 dates from June to August 1984. And though the drugs that had plagued their musical lives were still omnipresent, the dates proved a success, with old fans coming out of the woodwork to cheer the troupe on. It also piqued the interest of a man who arguably became their saviour.

John Kalodner, A&R man *par excellence* at Geffen Records, had watched Aerosmith's stumbling resurrection with some degree of hope. A massive fan of the band – 'I thought they were one of the greatest American rock bands ever' – and with a proven reputation for resuscitating acts declared dead, he felt there was still enough of the old fire left in the band to take a chance. After protracted talks with Tim Collins, who was eager for his troupe to have the best deal possible, Aerosmith found a new home at the rising Geffen. Now all that was left was the small matter of making an album.

To assist their recorded return, Aerosmith turned to the talents of Ted Templeman. Although there had been talk of Beatles producer George Martin twiddling the knobs, when the group heard at 1985's Grammy Awards that Templeman had expressed a serious interest in working with them, they knew they had found their man. Famous for his superb production duties with Van Halen, Ted Templeman's instinctive understanding of the hard rock sound was like a breath of fresh air to Aerosmith, and they re-doubled their writing efforts in anticipation of the union.

Choosing to record tracks at Fantasy Studios in Berkeley, California, with additional duties performed in New York's Power Station, work for 'Done With Mirrors' went quickly and well, with Templeman cleverly keeping the tapes running to capture live performances of the songs while the group were unaware of what was happening. It worked, with something like 'a song a day' being captured and an overall live ambience pervading the sound.

Aerosmith, for their sins, were also making the effort in their personal drug wars, battling desperately to avoid the substances that had been at the root of their downfall: 'Man, we were trying so hard,' said Tyler. 'On the way from the hotel we'd go to the health food shop and stock up on all the drugs they had that were legal, valerian root and all different kinds of sleepies. But then we'd go home and get shit-faced at the weekends.' Well, you can but try.

Engineered by Jeff Hendrickson and mastered by Howie Weinberg, 'Done With Mirrors' released in November 1985, garmered reasonable reviews and much back slapping from an industry that had written the band off as a spent force five years before. Nevertheless, listening to the album, many felt the old magic was missing. 'Let The Music Do The Talking' and 'Shame On You' rocked well enough, but other tracks sounded limp and unfinished, lacking that famous spark. However good the pairing of Templeman and Aerosmith had looked on paper, there was still a gaping hole in the sound that needed filling.

The cover, too, proved a disaster. Lacking their distinctive winged logo and with the group's name and album title printed backwards – a pun on the LP's name – it was difficult for buyers and shops alike to decipher whose product this was. Unsurprisingly, sales were sluggish, settling at around 400,000 units, millions away from those of 'Rocks' and 'Toys In The Attic'.

Still, they remained largely unrepentant with Perry scowling, 'So you have an album that doesn't do quite as well as the last one. Big fucking deal.' That said, Aerosmith were secretly disappointed at the lukewarm response to 'Done With Mirrors' and had learned the first great

lesson of their comeback – don't take anything for granted. There was much work still to be done.

NB: All tracks on this album are credited to the band as a whole.

LET THE MUSIC DO THE TALKING

Tumbling out of the speakers like a freight train, 'Let The Music Do The Talking' sees Aerosmith back in the saddle and taking on all comers. An upbeat, snare drum driven slice of American boogie, it's a fine reunion piece for the band and a definite statement of future intent. Originally written by Joe Perry for the 'Night In The Ruts' sessions, but brought with him to kick start his solo career (it's the title track of his first post-Aerosmith album), the song was re-worked for the 1984 comeback tour to include new lyrics, wheezy harmonicas and a smoking, slide guitar mid song breakdown.

'I think 'Let The Music' was the definitive Aerosmith song,' Steven Tyler told Mike Gitter of *Pulse* magazine in 1993, showing his obvious fondness for the number.

MY FIST, YOUR FACE

A simple, aggressive rock song with a thunderous drum sound compliments of producer Templeman, 'My Fist' could be Chuck Berry on steroids. Except of course, it isn't.

SHAME ON YOU

Funk rock, mined from the same source as 'Last Child', this is a real beauty from beginning to end. With the band following Perry's swirling stop/go riff, Tyler is free to flash his beat poet credentials to his heart's content: 'Seven on eleven, got to throw the dice/Am I in heaven, or am I in Miami Vice?'

With John Bonham-style drums, guitars sitting on the edge of feedback and a firebell to warn you there's smoke in the house, 'Shame On You' could have come straight off 'Rocks'.

THE REASON A DOG

While this mid-tempo ballad shows all the signs of being a cracker, it just never really comes alive. Let down especially by a middle section that sounds like it's still waiting to be finished, the overall impression is more that of a demo than a finished product.

Steven Tyler was irritated by the song's incompleteness, telling writer Mark Putterford, 'It just wasn't the best we could have made it.' Tom Hamilton fleshed out the singer's remarks in an interview with rock magazine *Music Connection* in 1987, succinctly nailing the malady that hangs over some of the album. 'We hadn't got used to one another again yet. The songs needed... to cook. We took 'em out of the oven too soon.' Half cooked , then.

SHELA

Another potential classic left cold in the middle. Starting promisingly with an unusual, syncopated riff that flicks snake-like around the drums, the song unfortunately fails to gel at any time.

Partial redemption comes via some real chance-taking leads from Joe and Brad, but even their combined talents can't pull the nose up.

GYPSY BOOTS

A catchy, if disjointed rocker reliant mainly on speed to make its point, 'Boots' sees Aerosmith pull off one of their great musical tricks – rescue by snare drum. With Perry scampering up and down the fretboard and Whitford and Hamilton giving frantic chase, it looks for a moment like everything will descend into aural chaos and then… *voilà!* Sanity is restored via Kramer's authoritative whip crack. Like a general rallying the troops, it's a miraculous stroke he pulls off again and again. (Listen to 'Live! Bootleg''s 'Sweet Emotion' or 'Night In The Ruts' 'Chiquita' for further proof.) To Joey Kramer then – human metronome and keen escapologist.

SHE'S ON FIRE

Ry Cooder's soundtrack for Southern Comfort seems to form the inspiration for this Dixie meets Middle Eastern showdown. Fine slide work from Perry and a smouldering vocal take from Tyler add the necessary sheen to raise the track to winning status.

THE HOP

Another fast and furious boogie hoe-down, 'The Hop' comes a little too close in track order to fellow sprinter 'Gypsy Boots' for its own good. Nevertheless, it's actually the better tune with Templeman accentuating each instrument nicely to enhance the overall tune. Present in the band's current live set, 'The Hop' would soon be replaced by newer material from 'Permanent Vacation'.

DARKNESS

Inexplicably left off the original album release, 'Darkness' is a real gem

Opening with a ghostly, beguiling piano highlighted by Kramer's ride-cymbal and Hamilton's intrusive high-end bass fills, Tyler soon stakes his claim to the song with a rich and strangely seductive vocal performance, full of pain and warped hope.

Changing gear several times and featuring a Perry solo so loud it literally breathes at one point, the song's spooky charm is the nearest Aerosmith have got to The X-Files. Released as a single (it didn't trouble the charts) if you don't have it on record it's actually worth seeking out for a listen. But don't say you weren't warned...

PERMANENT VACATION

(ORIGINAL RELEASE: AUGUST 1987; CD RELEASE GEFFEN 9241622)

In 1986 Aerosmith would achieve two much needed boosts to their career. An end to drug abuse, and another hit. Disappointed with the fair to middling sales of 'Done With Mirrors' and at last admitting to themselves that drugs were now blocking their creativity rather than enhancing it, the group checked into Pennsylvania's Caron Foundation Treatment Center to undergo rehabilitation. Sticking to the strict 12 step programme beloved of reformed users, they would emerge some months later, groggy but sober. The first time in 10 years.

The reward for their abstinence was swift. At the suggestion of their producer Rick Rubin (himself a big Aerosmith fan), wise-cracking rap act Run DMC were considering covering the old Aero hit 'Walk This Way' in the hope it would provide the crossover success they needed to break big in the American market. Yet, the mixes of the song needed something. Rubin, seizing a way forward, contacted Perry and Tyler with a view to adding their talents to the pot. In like Flynn, the Toxic Twins contributed guitar and vocals to the rappers' cuts and scratches and a huge hit was born. Scaling the Top 10 in America (No.4) and Great Britain (No.8),

it broke Run DMC worldwide and re-introduced Aerosmith to the critical youth market. The band were at last poised for their comeback.

Nevertheless, Geffen Records were still smarting from the unanticipated low key performance of 'Mirrors' on the chart and felt surgery was in order to fully resuscitate their patients. Enter the song doctors.

Holly Knight, Desmond Child and Jim Vallance, the tunesmiths who had given booster shots to the careers of Bon Jovi, Kiss and Bryan Adams (to name but a few), were hired to work with Aerosmith in the hope that the new record would be brimming with radio friendly hooks, catchy choruses and bankable singles. The operation would ultimately be a complete success.

At first however, news that the quintet were exploring new avenues for inspiration was greeted with cynicism, but Tyler bravely defended the decision telling *Sounds* in 1987, 'By writing with other people we just added another spice to the pot.' If 'Done With Mirrors'' half cooked feel was anything to go by, he was right. They needed hits, and if allowing external sources in provided them, then so be it.

Though initial recording for what would become 'Permanent Vacation' began in February 1987 with Rick Rubin at the helm (producing six demos with one, 'Love Me Like A Bird-dog', providing the embryo for 'Dude (Looks Like A Lady)', Rubin's tight scheduling meant that he simply didn't have time to finish the project. Nevertheless, any potential panic attacks were put firmly on hold when his replacement arrived. Bruce Fairbairn, an honest and upfront Canadian with an ear

for melody and a hard working production style, was just the catalyst Aerosmith needed to complete the task in hand.Moving to Little Mountain Sound Studios in Vancouver, discipline and control became the new drug-free Aerosmith watchwords, and with Fairbairn eliciting the same response in the group that Jack Douglas had created some twelve years earlier, new material flowed like water. Adding the contributions of Child, Vallance *et al,* Aerosmith had 28 songs to choose from by the end of the sessions, reluctantly whittling them down one by one to the final twelve that made the album. With fingers crossed and wishes made, 'Permanent Vacation' hit the stores replete with the band's old logo firmly emblazoned on the sleeve in August 1987.

The response was a unanimous thumbs up from critics and fans alike and the LP began to shift like hot cakes from the day of its release. The hungover feel of 'Mirrors' now a distant memory, 'Permanent Vacation' seemed to crackle with energy and humour, the sound youthful and vibrant all at once. Tracks such as 'Dude (Looks Like A Lady)' and 'Rag Doll' were easily as good as anything the group had recorded in their salad days, and with the new added commerciality (courtesy of Fairbairn, Vallance and friends), potential singles literally fought free from the LP's grooves. If a dissenting voice was heard to cry 'Sell out!' over the Tannoy system it was more than drowned by the roars of 'Welcome back' from the faithful.

With the triple whammy of 'Dude', 'Angel' and 'Rag Doll' roaring up the charts and cracking MTV wide open for the band, 'Permanent Vacation' shot past platinum status within weeks, eventually settling at around the 3 million mark as hit followed hit. Tyler was ecstatic with the success, declaring the record to be, 'The next logical step creatively from 'Rocks' and 'Toys In The Attic' albums of the Seventies.'

Against the odds, Aerosmith had pulled it off. And this time without a needle in sight. Emotive and vital, 'Permanent Vacation' is the Lazarus in their record

collection. And to think they were going to call it 'Monkey House'...

HEARTS DONE TIME
(Perry, Child)

A Perry/Child composition, 'Hearts Done Time' opens 'Permanent Vacation' grandly. Beginning in a swirling aural mist of air-raid sirens, grinding feedback and whalesong (two humpbacks taped especially for the occasion!), things quickly rev up with a vicious riff leading into the song proper. A guilty tale of back door love and cuckolded husbands, there are some cracking moments on show – Tyler opening his throat to hit those impossible high notes, Hamilton and Kramer securing a Siamese twin-like understanding of the rhythm, and a marvellous polyphonic guitar duel between Joe and Brad that threatens to descend into chaos several times, before the rest of the band provide a rescue. Simple, direct and devastatingly effective.

MAGIC TOUCH
(Tyler, Perry, Vallance)

Song doctor Jim Vallance's influence is all over this slim and frankly uninspired rock-by-numbers workout. Never a real Aerosmith track, 'Magic Touch' would sit more easily with Bryan Adams or Tina Turner at the helm. Lyrically nebulous, and with one eye constantly turned towards radio play, it half-heartedly limps along, only to be partially redeemed by an emotive middle eight, where Tyler seems to temporarily wake up and let rip with that voice.

RAG DOLL
(Tyler, Perry, Vallance, Knight)

Now this is more like it. Though co-writer Vallance is still present (with Holly Knight), this time his pop sensibilities do not drown Perry and Tyler's work. In fact, he enhances it, resulting in a marvellous commercial blues, brimming with life and cock-sure charm. Driven by an enormous drum sound courtesy of producer Bruce Fairbairn, cracking brass stabs from the

Margarita Horns and jaunty lap steel guitar work from Joe Perry, 'Rag Doll' swings in vintage Aerosmith fashion, allowing Steven Tyler to do the business. Bouncing across the track with lines such as, 'Get crazy on the moonshine' and, 'Tap dancing on a land mine', he's in inspirational form – but most especially at the song's Vaudeville finale, when scatting alongside a lonesome clarinet, he magically transports the listener to the heart of New Orleans.

SIMORIAH
(Tyler, Perry, Vallance)
For its first ten seconds or so, 'Simoriah' pleasingly recalls The Monkees' classic 'Last Train To Clarkesville' – all jangly guitars and youthful optimism – but, I'm afraid to say, it's all downhill from here. Never seeming to capitalise on its early promise and lacking a strong central melody, the tune meanders aimlessly, seemingly content to limp home on the back of a rather uninspired Perry solo. Did someone say the words 'Filler material'?

DUDE (LOOKS LIKE A LADY)

(Tyler, Perry, Child)

A tall story of a young man's surprise when he finds out that his new friend is packing more than a smile underneath her dress, 'Dude' is an infectious slice of Aerosmith at their very best – effortlessly surfing the waters between pop and rock without losing a drop of that much-needed credibility or humour in the process. Spinning around a simplistic double stop motif from Perry, the song is a joy from start to finish and cannily identifies what producer Fairbairn was bringing to the party. Instead of the band sounding blunt and metallic, he was imbuing them with a light, commercial, yet still steely touch that wailed 'Put me on the radio!' And it worked. 'Dude' would hit the Top 20 on both sides of the Atlantic, and provide as good an advertisement for 'Permanent Vacation' as they could get.

It's all here, Steven rocking like a mad dog, horns pumping along the melody line and a one-take Perry solo that raises the hairs on the back of your neck. As to whether the story in the song is true, you'd have to ask them.

ST JOHN
(Tyler)

A religious epic. Well, as close as Aerosmith will come to producing one anyway. 'St John' could, in fact, have come from the recording sessions of the band's first album, its loose, undisciplined structure reminiscent of former glories such as 'Moving Out' and 'One Way Street', and I must admit that it does sit uneasily with the other numbers present here. That said, it's still a cracker, with Tyler pontificating on abstinence, the Lord, and a link with The Twilight Zone late night TV, while the boys go to hell behind him in a rumble of white noise.

HANGMAN JURY
(Tyler, Perry, Vallance)

The standout track on 'Permanent Vacation' and a chance to travel into the Mississippi Delta with the band. A down home blues, complete with acoustic guitar, worn harmonica and rocking chair, Tyler got the idea for 'Hangman Jury' from hearing a snippet from a Taj Mahal record. Yet the phrase that so interested him – 'If I surely could' – had actually been borrowed by Taj from blues legend Leadbelly, who in turn had stolen it from an old cotton field chant sung by slaves in the deep South.

Whatever the history, in Tyler's hands these words would act as the inspiration for a remarkably powerful song detailing the murder of a wife at the hands of her husband, his dark reasoning for the deed and the terrible consequences to be faced:

'Poor boy sweatin' in the hot summer night/Hangman waitin' for the early morning light...'

With Steven's insightful and chilling vocal performance, and Joe's national steel invoking the ghost of Robert Johnson, the results are downright spooky. Created again for the stage, 'Hangman Jury' would be the live highlight of the 'Vacation' tour, and a testament to Aerosmith's skills at trying something different – and succeeding.

GIRL KEEPS COMING APART
(Tyler, Perry)

An up-tempo and horn driven tribute to the dance music that played a heavy influence in their formative years, Aerosmith again show their absolute mastery of the funk rock medium. Plaudits go in particular to Joey Kramer and Tom Hamilton for that clipped, edgy, rhythmic drive, and Brad Whitford for some wild lead guitar icing on the cake, though the late, great, Frank Zappa should also be mentioned for his lending the line 'She was buns up and kneeling' from his own 'Dinah – Moe Humm' to Steven Tyler to complete a particularly salty lyric.

ANGEL
(Tyler, Child)

The obligatory ballad. However, while Aerosmith have produced some good

ones over the years (see 'Seasons of Wither' and 'Dream On' for evidence), 'Angel' comes over as a rather leaden and lumpy affair, sounding rather too emotionally forced for its own good. Tyler remains fond of the song, recalling in US magazine the night it was written with Desmond Child: 'I was showing him the chords to 'Dream On'... and ten minutes later he was writing 'Angel'.' Slash from

Guns N' Roses called it, 'Too pop', and I've got to agree. Didn't stop it from becoming one of their biggest US singles though...

PERMANENT VACATION
(Tyler, Whitford)

Borrowing liberally from 'Day-O', 'Summertime Blues' and 'Montego Bay', the album's title track nevertheless rises above its influences quickly to become one of the more enjoyable moments on show. Built sturdily on a gunshot riff in D-major from Brad Whitford (whose bluesy economical lead lines are a joy) and with a great chorus, the essence is definitely on fun. Tyler paints vocal pictures of sun, sea and sin – with the drugs left well behind: 'My nose is clean and Lordie don't need no sedation.' With the band 80% clean – bassist Hamilton allegedly still using pot to relax – the singer wasn't afraid to let us know he was a changed man and enjoying it. Listening to those steel drums rattling away, and sample inserts of wild jungle noises everywhere, it isn't hard to join in.

I'M DOWN
(Lennon, McCartney)

Faithful re-working of the old Beatles chestnut, with Steven Tyler ripping up and down the ivories, and providing a passable vocal impression of Paul McCartney, had he chosen to gargle regularly with razor blades. Personally, I'd have preferred them to have had a crack at 'Revolution'.

THE MOVIE
(Tyler, Perry, Whitford, Hamilton, Kramer)

'Permanent Vacation''s concluding track, and a bit of an oddity. Best summed up as 'Music For Films', (its original intention), 'The Movie' is a rather doomy instrumental, invoking in the mind's eye a legion of monks pushing boulders up a steep hill. Moments of interest include a Gaelic voice-over, and some rather searing pinched harmonics from Perry's fretboard. An interesting experiment, if nothing else.

PUMP

(ORIGINAL RELEASE: SEPTEMBER 1989; CD RELEASE GEFFEN 9242542)

'**W**e really busted our nuts to do this record' – Joey Kramer. Keen to capitalise on the accomplishments of 'Permanent Vacation', and prove to the rock world that the album was more than a one-off, Aerosmith took the making of 'Pump' more seriously than any other album in their career.

Retaining the services of Bruce Fairbairn, whose re-vitalisation of their sound had played such a large part in the success of 'Permanent Vacation', the group buried themselves in pre-production duties at Rik Tinory's Studios in Cohasset, Massachusetts, for much of January and February of 1989, fine tuning new songs and collaborating with song doctors Jim Vallance ad Desmond Child once again for additional ideas. The sessions went well with 'Love In An Elevator' being one of many tunes born at RTS.

Ready now for the real thing, they flew to Little Mountain Sound Studios in Vancouver in March to begin the process of recording proper. But on arrival they found that Mötley Crüe, a quartet famous for their partying, were ensconced next door, working on tracks for what would become 'Dr Feelgood'. Any fears, however, that Aerosmith may have had about being lured into old ways were immediately placated as the Crüe, sick to death of ODs themselves, were equally concerned with staying on the wagon! Suffice to say, a firm friendship was struck, with the musicians more willing to pump iron and jog together than quaff liquor and fix up. Tyler even went so far as to add backing vocals to one of the LA quartet's songs. My, how times change...

With discipline high on the agenda and under the watchful eye of Fairbairn, recording for 'Pump' proved ruthless and efficient but not at the cost of creativity. While taking a break from studio duties, Aerosmith were introduced to a certain Randy Raine Reusch, local owner of a bizarre toy shop of exotic instruments. 'This guy had a room with hundreds, maybe thousands of them... big bamboo things, stuff made from human femurs,' recalled Steven. Startled by the other-worldly sounds the devices made, and eager to introduce a less commercial aspect to their sound (in response to the criticism levelled at 'Vacation''s change of their riff orientated sound), the band persuaded Reusch, 'To let us jam with them, and what we came up with, we used as interludes to tie the whole album together.' Adding African ritual music borrowed from Guns N' Roses' Izzy Stradlin and a water phone from band acquaintance Richard Waters, these interludes would form the backbone of 'Pump''s eclectic approach, and give the album a Native American ethnicity that distanced it from more standard fare.

With the remaining tracks completed by early summer, and backed with a unanimous thumbs up from Geffen's John

Kalodner (who had carefully monitored the album's progress), all that was left to do was give the baby a name. After hundreds of suggestions and much in-fighting, Brad Whitford's proposal won, and 'Pump' it was. Using a hilarious black and white photo of two trucks humping, from the Louisville Photographic Archive, as its sleeve, Aerosmith's latest effort landed in record stores in September 1989. And what an effort...

Termed 'a masterpiece of sexual innuendo and hellacious guitar' by *Rolling Stone* magazine, 'Pump' was truly special. Diverse, exquisitely performed and paced to perfection, the LP was Aerosmith's best team effort since the halcyon days of 'Rocks'.

Initially shipping platinum, sales would rise in excess of four million, aided by three US Top 10 singles, a much needed break into the European charts with 'Love In An Elevator' and a prestigious Grammy award for 'Janie's Got A Gun'.

Yet its most important act was to re-establish Aerosmith as elder statesmen of the groove, and leaders of an increasingly lucrative adult rock market. 'To have it again, and have it bigger than it was before... there is justice,' wryly observed Brad Whitford. Perfectly correct.

YOUNG LUST
(Tyler, Perry, Vallance)

In time-honoured tradition, Aerosmith choose to open their tenth studio album with a real shin kicker. 'Young Lust' – you can guess what it's about – is a cornucopia of raging Les Pauls, overwrought vocals and high octane drumming. All stops, starts and dead-drop rhythm, so fast is the pace set by the band it's almost over before it's begun. Fairbairn works everyone here, prising gold medal- winning performances especially from Tyler (who sounds twenty-one all over again) and Tom Hamilton, whose fluid, walking lines underpin the melodies so cleverly you remain largely unaware he's even there.

Horny, spirited and very funny, it's the best start to a 'Smith album since the last one.

F.I.N.E.
(Tyler, Perry, Child)

Or 'Fucked Up, Insecure, Neurotic and Emotional' as Aerosmith would have it. Quite simply their best moment since 'Rocks'' 'Lick And A Promise'. The result of a loose jam between Perry and Tyler, ('I sat down at the drums and hit this rhythm that came out of his guitar lick. One inspired the other,' the vocalist told Rolling Stones' David Fricke) F.I.N.E. doesn't so much rock as spontaneously combust. Guitars pile up, drumskins are broken and still Aerosmith keep coming, creating that 'see-saw' effect in the groove that remains uniquely theirs. Tyler, ever the Master of Ceremonies, simply rides the musical wave, spinning out his bawdy yarn over verse and chorus until he's ready to release that final killer punch-line, 'I hear that you're so tight your loving squeaks, And I'm ready, so ready.'

'There's a kind of swagger Aerosmith has when we're all together – that push-pull' Joe Perry once said, and 'F.I.N.E.' is what it is all about. Priceless.

LOVE IN AN ELEVATOR
(Tyler, Perry)

'Oh, Good Morning Mister Tyler, going... down?' With its 'woah yeah' verses, yodelling choruses and indubitably the best ending to an Aerosmith song ever, how could this fail to be a hit? An immodest tale of sex between floors, based, according to Steven, on his actual experiments in a hotel lift, 'Elevator' sees Aerosmith get commercial, but like 'Dude', without losing an ounce of credibility in the process. Loved by bikers, vicars and bored housewives alike, it took the band to the top of the charts on both sides of the Atlantic (No.5 USA, No.13 UK) and broke 'Pump' wide open to the all-important crossover market. Accompanied by a saucy, Benny Hill goes rock and roll video that netted the band MTV's 'Best Heavy Metal Video' and 'Viewers' Choice' awards, and the resurrection whch began with 'Permanent Vacation' was complete. Joe Perry: 'It was Spring when we cut the record. What can I tell ya?'

MONKEY ON MY BACK
(Tyler, Perry)

This harrowing tale of Tyler's chemical dependencies and his fight to be free recruits a supporting cast of fortune tellers, devils and dragons to make its point clear – clean up or face the consequences. Originating from a vicious slide guitar riff Perry had brought with him to the 'Pump' sessions, 'Monkey''s rhythmic gear shifts initially created problems for Joey Kramer, whose usually faultless stickwork wasn't locking into the time track in the way Tyler wanted it to. Several arguments later (one was particularly heated – see The Making Of Pump video for evidence), the pissed-off drummer would have his revenge by producing an astonishing, on-the-money take, which raised the song another level with its thunder.

Creating some controversy at the time of release for the use of the word 'fucking', Aerosmith's vocalist would justify his position thus: 'I use those words because they're very descriptive. It's my oranges and blacks and fuschias in my art. And no Tipper Gore, or any of those people are going to tell me I can't use that... If they agree with me that drugs are a big problem in the United States, and I ought to know, they're going to have to listen to me on how to tell my story.' Use of expletives or not, 'Monkey' is another of the album's highlights.

WATER SONG
(Uncredited)

A 10-second introduction into the wonders of the water-phone which, according to Tyler, is, 'Like a metal vase with rods sticking out... you fill it with water and swill them round a bit and... play it with a violin bow.' Cacophonous and unsettling, it's the perfect introduction to...

JANIE'S GOT A GUN
(Tyler, Hamilton)

In many ways the biggest success story on the album, 'Janie's Got A Gun' saw Aerosmith move into potentially uneasy water, and triumph despite the risks.

Initially inspired by an article Tyler had read in *Time* magazine concerning hand gun deaths, the singer soon connected the dots to child abuse, a subject that both shocked and frightened him. 'I heard this woman speaking about how many children are attacked by their fathers and mothers. It was fucking scary. I felt, man, I gotta sing about this.'

Taking an eerie Tom Hamilton bass-motif as his musical starting point, Tyler fashioned a frightening treatise on incest, despair and murderous retribution, combining exotic instrumentation, ghostly vocals and stabbing strings to enhance his chilling storyline. With a memorable, insistent chorus, a soaring electro-acoustic solo from Perry, the track was potentially a real epic – but would the subject matter make it unsuitable for a single release? John Kalodner, along with producer Fairbairn, the band's commercial ears, thought it was worth taking the chance and were proved right.

'Janie' would catapult in to No.4 in the Billboard charts and secure Aerosmith their first Grammy for Best

Rock Performance. A show-stopper live, with its moody lighting and impassioned Tyler vocal, 'Janie's Got A Gun' has helped the quintet move away from their sex-obsessed image (to a point), showing a serious side to their nature that was only previously hinted at in numbers such as 'Seasons Of Wither' and 'Nobody's Fault'.

DULCIMER STOMP
(Uncredited)

A joyous Cajun jaunt, all ringing harmonics and snappy percussion leading rather unevenly, it has to be said, into:

THE OTHER SIDE
(Tyler, Vallance)

A brass-driven rock and roll number written by Jim Vallance and Steven Tyler, and heavily reliant on The Rolling Stones for inspiration. A little too formulaic for its own good at times, the Margarita Horns chugging saxes and Tyler's multi-tracked harmonies do help infuse some life into

the proceedings, but the phrase 'light-weight' keeps coming to mind. A minor hit in the USA.

MY GIRL
(Tyler, Perry)

After attending a Keith Richards solo gig where 'The Human Riff' had played the old Stones fave 'Connection', Aerosmith came up with this tribute to Sixties British pop – all swinging beats, shifting keys and bouncy guitars. Some great salty lyrics from Tyler and a Chuck Berry inflected solo from Perry pull 'My Girl' out of novelty status, though it's still more Herman's Hermits than The Who.

DON'T GET MAD, GET EVEN
(Tyler, Perry)

Another Tyler/Perry original, this is a sleazy piece of blues-rock that more than tips its hat in Muddy Waters' direction. Slow and moody in the verses, and wild and chaotic on the choruses, its changes of pace are a sheer delight, giving Joey Kramer another chance to shine on the sticks.

Great harmonica and didgeridoo (!) from Tyler as well.

HOODOO
(Uncredited)

Native drums, half spoken words and droning off-kilter keyboards create a real slice of the old West, where you can almost see the Sioux going into battle. Aerosmith certainly seem to be getting the hang of indigenous music here. Leading into...

VOODOO MEDICINE MAN
(Tyler, Whitford)

With its reeling sustained guitar and wailing cut glass vocals, 'Voodoo' is another one of those marvellously heavy Brad Whitford songs that are crackling with atmosphere and tension. Featuring a career-best performance from Tom Hamilton (who had given himself tendonitis practising for 'Pump') and beautifully produced by Fairbairn, accenting every instrument, percussive tool, or

vocal inflection present, it's another
standout on an album of standouts.

WHAT IT TAKES
(Tyler, Perry, Child)
Desmond Child joins Perry and Tyler on
the songwriting team for this gentle country ballad, which scaled the US charts to
No.9 in April 1990. With a desperately
poignant lyric full of regret, and a highly
emotive Leslie guitar solo from Perry, the
hankies are always near. Like The Beatles
colliding with Tammy Wynette, this is a
song for lovers everywhere.

UNTITLED
(Uncredited)
'Pump' ends with a Zydeco stomp, dul-
cimers and jaw harps spelling out the
melody as an insistent bass drum keeps
the beat. Played by Perry and Tyler,
images of the Bayou flood the mind.

GET A GRIP

(ORIGINAL RELEASE: APRIL 1993; CD RELEASE GEFFEN GED 2444)

Work on the follow up to the mighty 'Pump' began in earnest shortly after Christmas 1991, with Aerosmith booking into Los Angeles' A&M Studios. Though producer Bruce Fairbairn returned for a third time, there were some changes on the engineering front, with new boy David Thoener replacing band regular Mike Fraser, and Ken Lomas being promoted from second engineer's duties to senior status. Another new face, Brendan O'Brien, would also take over from the talented Fraser who had doubled on the mixing desk. Nevertheless, despite all the reshuffles, spirits were high and recording was expected to go quickly.

To a point it did. Within two months Aerosmith had an album's worth of material on tape including versions of 'Eat The Rich', 'Amazing' and what would become the title track of the LP. However, the general feeling was that the dynamism that had been present on their two previous albums was missing. Steven Tyler: 'When we stepped back and looked at the big picture, we weren't sure if this was what we wanted to follow 'Pump'... the question was not whether the songs were any good but rather did we have the time to make them better? We decided to make the time.'

Returning then to Joe Perry's home studio, The Boneyard, where many of their new ideas had been generated, Aerosmith worked with additional engineer Dave Frangioni to fine tune existing tracks, and try and create some new ones. The sessions were a success with several songs emerging including one of the album's highlights, 'Gotta Love It'. Confidence largely restored, the team hastily reconvened at Vancouver's Little Mountain Sound Studios (thus avoiding further work in LA, where the riots that had formed the background of initial sessions were still sporadically raging) to finish the job. By Winter 1992, it was, as they say, 'In the can'.

Unveiled the following Spring, the word that best described the album was 'patchy'. Though more upbeat than 'Pump' and certainly their most song orientated release yet, 'Get A Grip' still struggled hard to grab the listener, relying more on style than content to persuade. As usual there were highlights, with the manic energy of 'Eat The Rich' and the unctuous 'Can't Stop Messin'' leading the pack. And it must be added that the sophisticated balladry of 'Livin' On The Edge' and 'Cryin'' would have graced any LP with their presence. Yet despite (or perhaps because of) the efforts of no less than eight song doctors and extensive re-recording, the overall effect lacked focus with pacing uneven and little swagger to be found.

It wasn't all doom and gloom though, 'GAG' did have a crisp, biting edge to its sound (thanks largely to the use of vintage amplification in recording), and Steven Tyler's voice had frankly never sounded better: rich, evocative and glori-

ously melodic, its soaring authority saved many tunes from a lingering death. But however you cut the mustard, it seemed that Aerosmith's latest commercial evolution was now sapping the sheer spirit of their Seventies incarnation, and replacing it instead with technique.

Still, if 'Get A Grip' had been Aerosmith's weakest moment since 'Done With Mirrors', it certainly didn't stop the public from buying it. With the kick off single 'Livin' On The Edge' coasting into the US Top 5 and several other subsequent hits, sales would rocket to an unprecedented 10 million units – (with 5 million of these from territories outside North America), and provide Aerosmith with their first ever No.1 placing on the US Billboard album chart. In a world rocked by the searing nihilism of Nirvana and Pearl Jam, this was no mean feat.

Yet as 'Get A Grip' sold by the truck-load, it was surprisingly announced that Aerosmith were to depart from Geffen Records, and return to their former home at Columbia/Sony, in a record breaking deal worth a reported 30 million dollars. In the move, the band would regain much control over their lucrative back catalogue, and receive the added bonus of a highly preferential royalty rate for all future releases on the label.

Though the move seemed at first ungracious, in consideration of the time and money Geffen had spent on bringing the band back from the brink, in the cold light of day, it made perfect business sense – Aerosmith were no longer green youngsters, deliriously happy to have their names emblazoned on a LP. They were seasoned veterans of the rock and roll wars, with families and children to support, and if Columbia were willing to up the stakes, so much the better. Still, with only a greatest hits album and live record left to contractually console him, Aerosmith's Geffen guru, John Kalodner, must have been crying great big wet tears into that beard.

Corporate business shenanigans aside, one thing was certain – Aerosmith had retained their wicked sense of humour. Cutting a welcome swathe through the images of plaid shirts and sullen faces staring from record shop racks, 'Get A Grip''s cover summed up the band's high spirits.

Faithful in tone to its predecessor 'Pump''s salty photography, the sleeve

featured a close-up of a cow's hind quarters branded with the band's logo and an earring decoratively placed through one of its udders. And though Tyler was at pains to point out that Hugo Syme's computer generated cow suffered no pain, the Devilish imagery was a welcome reminder that under that new skin of clean living, commercial endeavour and financial acumen, five horny little hearts were still beating...

INTRO
(Uncredited)
A cod-rap from Tyler, replete with African chants and a snatch of 'Walk This Way' paves the way for...

EAT THE RICH
(Tyler, Perry, Vallance)
From the opening bars, it's clear that this record was cut to disc loud. The smooth polished edges of 'Permanent Vacation' and 'Pump' are abandoned in favour of a more raw, abrasive sound – bone dry, with the guitars to the fore. As a result, 'Eat The Rich' is initially a shock to the system but not an unpleasant one.

Following with tradition, this is a thumping, anarchic affair, fast-paced and mercifully free of pretension. Commerciality is retained however, with a big, radio-friendly chorus and tight snappy drums. (In fact, a troupe of Polynesian log drummers were hauled in to add a little extra oomph to the proceedings).

Standard Aerosmith kick off then, but it is nice to hear Perry, who seemed to have passed from lead guitar innovator to classicist in the Geffen years, let fly with a frankly inspired solo that recalls the heady freedom of his 'Project' days.

Surprisingly released as a single, (presumably because hit master Jim Vallance had had a hand in writing it) it failed to dent the upper reaches of the charts on either side of the Atlantic.

GET A GRIP
(Tyler, Perry, Vallance)
The title track; and a real let down.

Basically a collection of guitar hooks that never once threaten to mesh, Tyler has to really fight here to extract a tune. Bereft of their usual swing, and sounding frankly laboured in parts, all Fairbairn's sonic trickery can't save 'Get A Grip' from sounding like Aerosmith parodying... Aerosmith.

FEVER
(Tyler, Perry)

Opening with Perry's echoed squeals and a Cossack-like backing vocal: 'Hey! Hey! Hey! Hey!' this soon warms up into a slight, if likeable country boogie, chords and keys shifting at regular intervals to keep up the pace. Splendid harmonies from Tyler ensure the melody is never far away – unlike 'Get A Grip' – and the overall effect is that of a band enjoying themselves. C&W superstar Garth Brooks, a man usually more at home with gentle ballads, would cover the tune with great success, proving once and for all that there is a rocker's heart beating under that cowboy shirt.

LIVIN' ON THE EDGE
(Tyler, Perry, Hudson)

A cacophonous, jack-booted ballad, co-written by Tyler and Perry with the assistance of Mark Hudson, 'Livin' On The Edge' is arguably 'GAG''s finest song and again sees the band cautiously dip their toe in social issues. Inspired by Aerosmith's proximity to the Los Angeles riots while recording part of the album, Steven's lyrics are awash with frightening images of a world gone mad, content to slip into hatred and anarchy. With Perry and Whitford's screeching, edge of feedback guitars and a slowly descending, multi-tracked chorus providing suitable musical drama, 'Edge' teeters on epic status for most of its six minutes. Scoring high placings on the American and British charts as a single, and also winning a Grammy in 1994 for Best Rock Performance by a Band, it has become a central point in their concert performance, though recreating the orchestrated magnificence of the studio cut has always proved difficult.

'Lennon was in the room when we

came up with that song,' said the justly proud Tyler. However, with 'Heart Full Of Soul' guitar riffery, perhaps the ghost of Yardbird Keith Relf also made a supernatural visit.

FLESH
(Tyler, Perry, Child)

More parody. This impotent ode to the libido from Tyler, Perry and Desmond Child is at best pitiful. Disjointed, tuneless and criminally lacking in ideas, it's astonishing to believe that it made the album at all. Aerosmith have never sunk so low.

WALK ON DOWN
(Perry)

A gritty, straight ahead rocker, penned and sung by Joe. Never the greatest of vocalists, he substitutes attitude for tunefulness here, sneering his way through the verse before fellow toxic twin Tyler helps out on the bruising chorus. Suitably in keeping with the guitarist's moody image and packed with some truly vicious solo flights, 'Walk On Down' is a refreshing change to the more commercial moments on the album. Farmed into their current live set to spotlight Perry, Tyler was initially hesitant to include it on the album but soon found the track had relative advantages: 'It's a staunch fucking thing, y'know? Plus, it gives me time to take a piss in the middle of the show!'

SHUT UP AND DANCE
(Tyler, Perry, Blades, Shaw)

Co-written with Jack Blades and Tommy Shaw from the Metal-Lite Damn Yankees, 'Shut Up And Dance' is a rather too formulaic power pop jaunt, saved largely by a 'sod the radio' middle track freakout and some humorous lyrics from Tyler – 'Sex is like a gun. You aim, you shoot, you run.' One of the last songs recorded for the album, and eventually released as a single to coincide with its inclusion in Wayne's World II, its effect after repeated listenings can be wearing.

CRYIN'
(Tyler, Perry, Rhodes)

A crackling, Nashville-tinged ballad with Taylor Rhodes sharing the songwriting credits with Tyler and Perry this time, 'Cryin'' proved a massive hit single, breaking the album wide open for world wide sales and copping the band three prestigious MTV Awards for the accompanying video – Best Video Of The Year, Viewers' Choice and Best Group Video – though cynics might suggest that the gorgeous Alicia Silverstone's appearance in the promo might have had something to do with it...

Alternating between soft, wistful passages and Hammond organ-powered choruses, the song features Steven's best vocal on 'GAG', his harmonies effortlessly linking the myriad chord changes into a wonderful whole. Aching harmonicas, mournful brass and Joe's best impression of Bluesbreakers-period Clapton, it's all there. And yet unbelievably, the song was rehearsed for only two days before recording, the general feeling

being that it wasn't worthy of inclusion. Strange indeed, if you consider that 'Flesh' made it onto the album with no questions asked.

GOTTA LOVE IT
(Tyler, Perry, Hudson)

This charming 'psychedelic sandwich' covered in backwards tape loops and clever sound F/X bows its head to Aerosmith's more exotic influences, namely 'Sgt Pepper' period Beatles. Featuring star solo turns from Brad Whitford and Tom Hamilton, 'Gotta Love It' was nearly lost due to technical hitches while recording. To save the day, the original demo was flown in from Perry's home studio, The Boneyard, and worked up to speed. A weird and welcome distraction.

CRAZY
(Tyler, Perry, Child)

Another hit single, and a fine companion piece to 'Cryin''. Again, country music is the primary influence on this mellow love song, made interesting with its mandolin trills and achy breaky harmonica interludes. Tyler once said that if he were ever to cut a solo album, it would be full of lonesome cowboy songs. Under that definition then, 'Crazy' would surely qualify.

LINE UP
(Tyler, Perry, Kravitz)

And it's welcome back to the Margarita Horns. A mid-tempo stomper, co-written with band friend and Seventies retro king Lenny Kravitz, 'Line Up' combines Stax soul and brassy R&B to make its mark. Pumping basslines from Hamilton and a spider-like slide guitar from Perry move the track along, but it's Tyler's lyrical gusto that ultimately pulls 'Line Up' above ordinary status.

CAN'T STOP MESSIN'
(Tyler, Perry, Blades, Shaw)

Whistling in on more backwards echo, this cracking little rock song finds the band in down and dirty mode, all bumps, grinds and sneers. A solo turf war between Whitford and Perry helps keep up the pressure in the middle section and Tyler's bluesy harmonica fills are always welcome. Reared in the same stable as 'S.O.S.' and 'Rats In The Cellar'.

AMAZING
(Tyler, Supa)

The product of a collaboration between Tyler and old pal Richie 'Lightnin' Strikes' Supa (who appears on piano here), 'Amazing' is the frank and redemptive tale of Steven's crawl from the pharmaceutical wreckage towards the light of sobriety. Superbly produced and mixed by Fairbairn and secret weapon Brendan O'Brien, the track builds from a simple piano and cello figure to full blown orchestral madness, with Perry bringing matters to a shattering climax courtesy of his Les Paul. Though lyrically cloying at times in its earnestness, the sheer emotional weight of Tyler's performance is hard to fault, and in ways it's as good a picture as you'll ever get of Aerosmith's

moment of clarity and subsequent resurrection. Keep an ear out for ex-Eagle Don Henley on backing vocals, as well as some crafty studio tomfoolery at the song's conclusion.

BOOGIE MAN
(Tyler, Perry)

A Grammy-nominated instrumental, heavy on atmosphere and perfectly described by its title. The result of an impromptu jam between Perry and Tyler, its shimmering guitars and clanking keyboards would perfectly suit the soundtrack of a horror movie.

'A tip of my hat to The Shadows and Peter Green,' remarked Joe Perry.

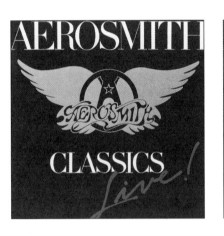

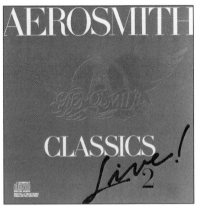

LIVE ALBUMS, GREATEST HITS AND ANTHOLOGIES

Various compilations, anthologies and live sets exist as a supplement to Aerosmith's studio catalogue and a review of each collection follows.

CLASSICS LIVE!
(Original release: 1986; CD Release Columbia/CBS 4749712)

Plucked from the Columbia vaults to cash in on Aerosmith's 1986 commercial success with Run DMC on 'Walk This Way', 'Classics Live!' is a poor representation of the band in concert, dating from 1977-1983. Allegedly touched up by then ex-group member Jimmy Crespo and singer/guitarist Adam Bomb, not even their efforts can disguise the tired performances present here.

In fact, it's hard to believe that anyone could have sanctioned the release of the version of 'Train Kept A Rollin'' that appears on this CD. With Tyler at half mast and a guitar solo that redefines the term 'tuneless', it's bloody awful. Only

'Three Mile Smile/Reefer Headed Woman' and 'Kings And Queens' show any sign of the old party spirit. Slight relief comes with the inclusion of a gorgeous studio version of the bitter sweet 'Major Barbara', but frankly it's not enough. One to avoid.

CLASSICS LIVE ! 2
(Original release: 1987; CD Release Columbia/CBS 4600372)

Much better. Eager to redeem themselves after the poorly received 'Classics Live!', Aerosmith co-operated with their old record company on this second live set, contributing their own collection of concert recordings to ensure quality control. The result is eight cracking performances with the high points including a powerhouse 'Movin' Out' and a roof raising 'Last Child', drawn from a Boston gig in 1984. Tom Hamilton even has the pleasure of being serenaded with 'Happy Birthday' by the entire crowd of their hometown's Orpheum Theater.

Graced with the additional delights of an extended 'Same Old Song And Dance', and a skittering 'Let The Music Do The Talking', this Paul O'Neill produced concert set is in many ways as likeable as 'Live! Bootleg'.

AEROSMITH'S GREATEST HITS

(Original release: 1980; CD Release Columbia/CBS 4607032)

Released in 1980 to plug the gap between albums and subsequently shifting over four million copies, this is a workman-like collection of Aerosmith's more commercial moments. All the hits are here,' Walk This Way', 'Sweet Emotion', 'Dream On', plus a smoky studio version of The Beatles' ,'Come Together',

recorded especially for the soundtrack of the dreadful Robert Stigwood film *Sgt. Pepper's Lonely Hearts Club Band*, in which the group played villains. All in all then, a good introduction to classic 'Smith.

Rumour has it that Joe Perry was so out of it at the time of 'Greatest Hits' release that he only became aware of its existence when a fan approached him in a supermarket asking him to autograph a copy!

BIG ONES

(Original release: 1994; CD Release Geffen GED 24546)

Another greatest hits package, this time focusing on the band's Geffen years, with all the recent singles such as 'Livin' On The Edge' and 'Janie's Got A Gun' present. However, there are some additional tracks on the disc not so widely available to tempt you into buying: 'Walk On Water' – a fine 'up and at 'em' rocker, produced by Michael Beinhorn and reminiscent of the rollin' and tumblin' grandeur of Seventies Aerosmith; 'Blind Man' – country-inflected power pop with a cracking Tyler harmony vocal and a spiritually uplifting chorus; 'Deuces Are Wild' (previously available on 'The Beavis And Butthead Experience') – a breezy, radio-friendly slice of commerciality; and a live version of 'Dude' that quite literally smokes. If you don't own 'Permanent Vacation', 'Pump' or 'Get A Grip', it's a good starter.

GEMS
(Original release: 1988; CD Release Columbia/CBS 4632242)

Issued by Columbia in 1988 to capitalise on Aerosmith's resurrection with 'Permanent Vacation' and 'Pump', 'Gems' is a surprisingly good compilation album concentrating on the band's harder side. Tracks include the brilliant 'Lick And A Promise', 'No Surprize', Brad Whitford's crunch festival 'Nobody's Fault' and band mascot 'Train Kept A Rollin''. One additional bonus is a studio version of Richie Supa's 'Chip Away The

Stone'. A recommended purchase for those Aerosmith fans who, like Joe Perry, think the ballads sometimes get in the way of the guitars.

BOX OF FIRE
(Box Set. Original release: 1994; Columbia CXK 66687)

A collection of all Aerosmith's Columbia/CBS albums from 1973's self-titled début to 1981's 'Rock in A Hard Place' (plus 1986/1987's 'Classics Live! I' and 'II', 1980's 'Greatest Hits' and 1988's 'Gems') this is a beautifully packaged memento designed for the Aerosmith completist. All 12 compact discs present are restored to their original master quality by the use of 20-bit digital mapping (and doesn't it make a difference), and the set also includes a bonus 5-track CD containing rare material such as the band's version of the old rave-up 'Rocking Pneumonia And The Boogie Woogie Flu' (first made available on the movie soundtrack for Less Than Zero), Dave Thoener's 1991 remix of the

flag-flying 'Sweet Emotion' and the 'Draw The Line' period instrumentals 'Subway' and 'Circle Jerk'. However, the hidden treasure on this CD is easily the symphonic version of 'Dream On', recorded at Boston's Orpheum Theater for MTV's 10th anniversary celebrations - with a full orchestra conducted by Michael Kamen behind it, the song takes on a soaring, emotional quality that sadly the restrictions of budget when originally recorded could not give it.

With original full sleeve jackets present, and a host of additional photographs of the band, this is certainly the most comprehensive Aerosmith set available, but with a hefty price tag, unfortunately it's out of many fans' reach. Limited number available.

ANTHOLOGY - AEROSMITH
(Original release: 1988; CD Release Raw Power RawCD 037)
A lovingly compiled career retrospective of the band's Columbia years, this is in many ways the best collection on the market outside of 'Pandora's Box'. It features all the great moments, plus a varied dip into lesser-known diamonds such as 'Coney Island White Fish Boy (Bone To Bone)', 'Sight For Sore Eyes' and Joe Perry's iconoclastic 'Bright Light Fright'. An example of good taste is the inclusion of the pneumatic concert version of 'Walk This Way' from 'Live! Bootleg'. With 18 tracks (21 if you buy the album version – RAW LP037), a concise, yet insightful appreciation of the band by Ian R. Attewell, and a running time of 74 minutes, it's the pick of the litter.

PANDORA'S BOX

(ORIGINAL RELEASE: 1991; CD RELEASE COLUMBIA CD 4692932)

To many Aerosmith fans, 'Pandora's Box' must seem like manna from heaven. A painstakingly assembled 52-track 3CD box set chock full of previously unreleased material, alternative and/or live takes of crowd favourites and a superbly informative 64-page booklet packed with rare facts and photographs, it's an absolute delight to wallow in, and worthy of several evenings' listening.

Inspired by compilations such as Led Zeppelin's 'Re-Masters' and Eric Clapton's 'Crossroads' and compiled with the full co-operation of the band (who were after all about to re-sign with the label at time of release), Columbia have gathered here the most definitive Aerosmith collection bar none. Scouring vaults for concert tapes, accessing early studio demos of songs that were destined to become classics, and digging out a plethora of never before heard tracks that rightly deserved to see light of day, 'Pandora's Box' documents the group from their earliest origins to 1982's 'Rock In A Hard Place', finding time to include a number of contributions from Joe Perry

and Brad Whitford's solo albums as well. Whether a completist eager to obtain the group's scorching cover of The Beatles' 'Helter Skelter' from 1975 or a casual listener trying to ascertain what all the fuss is about, this compilation is eager to serve.

Previously unavailable tracks are as follows:

WHEN I NEEDED YOU
(1966) (Tyler)

Tyler's pre-Aerosmith ensemble Chain Reaction recorded this Yardbirds inspired rave-up, available here in its original form. Strange to note that the then young vocalist had not yet found his now trademark holler, sounding positively muted in comparison to later glories. Also features Steven on drums.

ON THE ROAD AGAIN
(1972) (Unknown)

Omitted from the band's self-titled début album, this mid-paced rock and roller, whilst not riveting, is spiky enough to pique the interest.

RATTLESNAKE SHAKE
(1971) (Griffith, Gilmore)

The old Fleetwood Mac slow burn special and proud father to Aerosmith's 'Rats In The Cellar'. Taken from a live WKRQ Cincinnati radio broadcast in 1971.

KRAWHITHAM
(1977) (Kramer, Whitford, Hamilton)

A menacing instrumental written by Kramer, Whitford and Hamilton to kill time during Perry and Tyler's 'recreational' breaks while recording 1977's 'Draw The

Line'. Doesn't take much to figure out how it got its title, though.

ALL YOUR LOVE
(1977) (Rush)

Again from the 'Draw The Line' sessions, this is a lusty version of the Otis Rush original, replete with clever tempo changes, a superlative Tyler vocal and fine drumming from Kramer.

SOUL SAVER
(1975) (Tyler, Whitford)

Only 53 seconds long, but this sinewy riff was enough to inspire 'Rocks'' most vicious moment – 'Nobody's Fault'.

I LIVE IN CONNECTICUT
(1974) (Tyler, Perry)

Another snippet, this time from the 'Night In The Ruts' pre-production rehearsals at the Wherehouse in Waltham, Massachusetts. Went on to become that album's 'Three Mile Smile'.

LET IT SLIDE
(1979) (Tyler, Perry)

The instrumental foetus for 'Night In The Ruts'' glorious 'Cheesecake', this sees Perry and Co. honing his about-to-be-classic slide guitar riff into workable shape.

DOWNTOWN CHARLIE
(1978) (Aerosmith)

A 'drunken jam' led by Brad Whitford's buzzsaw guitar, everyone sounds as if they're enjoying this Chuck Berry approved free-for-all.

SHIT HOUSE SHUFFLE
(1979) (Perry)

The gem that would become Perry's finest solo moment, 'South Station Blues'. Thirty-five seconds long, but worth inclusion just for that dragging shuffle beat.

Marvellous title, as well.

RIFF & ROLL
(1981) (Tyler, Crespo)

Soul and blues mesh nicely together on this outtake from the 'Rock in A Hard Place' sessions. Sadly, this radio-friendly track, with its instantly memorable guitar hook was never developed beyond demo stage.

HELTER SKELTER
(1975) (Lennon, McCartney)

Manic cover of The Beatles original, covered in scratchy guitars and yelping vocals.

Alternative Takes:

MOVIN' OUT
(1972) (Tyler, Perry)

While more disciplined than the version that made the début album, it lacks the ragged charm of the take that everyone has become familiar with.

LAST CHILD
(1976) (Tyler, Whitford)

Remix of the 'Rocks' original with Whitford's biting solo now well to the fore. A little longer as well.

DRAW THE LINE
(1977) (Tyler, Perry)

Remix of the Tyler/Perry classic, this time emphasising the song's rhythmic drive.

MAJOR BARBARA
(1971) (Tyler)

Melancholic and touching, 'Barbara' is a song for true romantics. However, the better version still exists on 'Classics Live!'.

CHIP AWAY THE STONE
(1978) (Supa)

Alternative take of the hit single that never was. And the question is why?

Solo Album Additions on 'Pandora's Box':

SOUTH STATION BLUES
(1981) (Perry)

Drawn from Perry's second solo album, 'I've Got The Rock N' Rolls Again', a more moody slice of downtrodden blues rock is hard to find.

SHARPSHOOTER
(1981) (Whitford, St.Holmes)

The flagship number from his solo collaboration with Derek St Holmes this single-handedly proves Brad Whitford is a great lead guitar player in his own right, as well as a capable songwriter.

Live tracks on 'Pandora's Box': 'Walkin' The Dog' - live radio broadcast from WKRQ Cincinnati (1971) - particularly recommended/'Write Me A Letter' - Boston (1976)/'I Wanna Know Why' - Texxas Jam (1978)/'Big Ten Inch Record' - Texxas Jam (1978)/'Kings And Queens' - Boston (1978)/'Adam's Apple' - Indianapolis - (1977)/'Lord Of The Thighs' - Texxas Jam (1978).

Other Songs Available On 'Pandora's Box': 'Make It', 'One Way Street', 'Mama Kin', 'Same Old Song And Dance', 'Train Kept A Rollin'', 'Seasons Of Wither', 'Dream On', 'Pandora's Box', 'Toys In The Attic', 'Round And Round', 'You See Me Crying', 'Sweet Emotion', 'No More No More', 'Walk This Way', 'Rats In The Cellar', 'Nobody's Fault', 'Lick And A Promise', 'Critical Mass', 'Milk Cow Blues', 'Three Mile Smile', 'Cheese Cake', 'Bone To Bone (Coney Island White Fish Boy)', 'No Surprize', 'Come Together', 'Jailbait', and 'Back In The Saddle'.

An abridged 12-track version of 'Pandora's Box', 'Pandora's Toys', exists both as a single CD (Columbia CD 4769562) and limited edition CD (10,000 only) in a wooden presentation box with numbered certificate, patch, sticker and bonus 'Story Of Aerosmith' CD Single.

VIDEOS AND MISCELLANEOUS GEMS WORTH SEEKING OUT

VIDEOS

Six Aerosmith videos are currently available on the retail market.

AEROSMITH VIDEO SCRAPBOOK

(Hendring HEN2105; running time: 54 minutes)

An entertaining, if not particularly innovative video documentary, drawn largely from live performances of the band during the Seventies. (Choice numbers here include 'Same Old Song And Dance' and 'Adam's Apple'). Things become markedly better though, with the inclusion of Eighties promos for 'Chiquita' and the hilarious 'Lightning Strikes', which sees Aerosmith don quiffs and biker jackets to emulate a street gang. I carry the sight of Steven Tyler's 'DA' to my grave.

AEROSMITH LIVE - TEXXAS JAM 78

(CMV Enterprises CMV 49013-2: running time: 50 minutes)

A straightforward concert film of the band's headline appearance at the Texxas World Music Festival in 1978 (with over 150,000 fans attending), this captures a tired and wasted Aerosmith going through the motions, with only the occasional smattering of brilliance to see them through. Tyler especially seems in poor health, rooted to one spot for much of the gig with only a mike stand for support, his usually superlative voice unable to hit those all important high notes. Well known Animal Rights activist Ted Nugent lends a guitar hand to the encore 'Milk Cow Blues', but this video is sometimes no more than harrowing evidence of a group at war with itself.

AEROSMITH - THINGS THAT GO PUMP IN THE NIGHT

(Geffen 759938172-3; running time: 45 minutes)

A slight but impressive video, featuring uncensored versions of 'Love In An Elevator', 'Janie's Got A Gun' and two alternative shoots for 'What It Takes'. 'Janie's Got A Gun' is the standout, a dark and disturbing affair directed by David ('Seven') Fincher, its incestuous theme is a 'movie of the week' in its own right. With the addition of saucy behind-the-scenes footage and brief interviews with the band, not at all bad.

AEROSMITH - THE MAKING OF PUMP

(CMV Enterprises CMV49064-2; running time: 110 minutes)

They don't come much better than this. A candid and at times highly charged documentary which reveals how the ground breaking 'Pump' was written and recorded, this takes the viewer into the heart of the Aerosmith machine – warts

and all. Particular highlights include the unexpurgated evolution of 'Love In An Elevator', the musical anarchy of a Perry/Whitford guitar war and an extremely uncomfortable 'fly on the wall' view of a Tyler/Kramer argument that pulls no punches. Interspersed with comprehensive interviews with each band member, and featuring insights from producer Bruce Fairbairn and 'sixth-ear' John Kalodner, The Making of Pump is a cut above most other music videos on release.

AEROSMITH - BIG ONES YOU CAN LOOK AT

(Geffen GEFV39546; running time: 100 minutes)

A faithful compilation of all Aerosmith's video hits, from the Benny Hill- like shenanigans of the Marty Callner produced 'Elevator'; to the award winning dark images of 'Livin' On The Edge'. The real bonus here though is the inclusion of the promos for 'Cryin'', 'Crazy' and 'Amazing'; little vignettes of teenage life and love, they all feature the impressive talents of actress Alicia Silverstone, whose lethal combination of earthy charisma and doe-eyed beauty ensured maximum rotation on youth-obsessed MTV. (Actor Stephen Dorff and Steven Tyler's own daughter, the startling Liv, also make appearances in 'Amazing' and 'Crazy' respectively.)

More behind the scenes footage and a bewildering array of unintentionally funny foreign interviews add to the entertainment quota.

N.B. Also popping up in 'Big Ones You Can Look At' is a split second cameo from Bay Watch Queen Pamela Anderson, who appears in 'Blind Man''s video as a scantily clad nurse. Rumours however, that her fleeting presence was enough to give the compilation its name remain unfounded.

Also available is AEROSMITH - 3x5, a compilation of 'Permanent Vacation' film clips containing the promos for 'Dude (Looks Like A Lady)', 'Rag Doll' and 'Angel'. (Not commercially available in the UK.)

And for anyone wanting to learn how to play 'Walk This Way', 'Back In The Saddle' and other Aerosmith songs, there is a guitar instructional video from Star Songs doing the rounds. However, please note, the band do not appear in it.

MISCELLANEOUS GEMS WORTH SEEKING OUT

In addition to their main album catalogue, there exist a number of rarer Aerosmith recordings which may be of interest. The list below, while by no means comprehensive, features some of the better moments in no particular order. Again, bootlegs not considered.

VACATION CLUB

(Original release 1988; Geffen CD 22P2-2132)

Released for the Japanese market as an accompaniment to 'Permanent Vacation', this five track CD features extended and a capella versions of 'Dude', an AOR mix of 'Angel', a 'twelve inch' mix of 'Rag

Doll' and the added bonus of corking country rocker 'Once Is Enough'. Available on import only, and very expensive as well.

CALIFORNIA JAM TWO
(Original release 1978; LP
Columbia/CBS 88318)

A two record concert set from 1978's Cal Jam Two, Aerosmith appear on three cuts - 'Chip Away The Stone', 'Draw The Line' and 'Same Old Song And Dance'. All performances are excellent, if a little frayed around the edges. Other artists featured on the album include Santana, Heart, Frank Marino and Mahogany Rush.

INTERVIEW PICTURE DISC
(Original release 1988; Baktabak
Records BAK2091)

An interview picture disc, with Aerosmith in conversation *circa* 1985. Revealing, if a little dry at times.

LIMITED EDITION HITS EP - DONINGTON 1990
(Original release 1990;
Geffen GEF 79TG)

A twelve inch EP, released to commemorate Aerosmith's 1990 Donington appearance, this features a club mix of 'The Other Side' backed by 'Love In An Elevator', 'Dude (Looks Like A Lady)' and 'Walk This Way' (edit) with Run DMC.

DARKNESS MAXI SINGLE
(Original release 1985;
Geffen GEF 020501)

Features the studio version of 'Darkness', originally omitted from LP version of 'Done With Mirrors', plus live versions of 'The Hop', 'My Fist, Your Face' and 'She's On Fire'. Again, the live performances here are excellent, particularly 'Fire' where Perry shines on slide duties.

AIR AMERICA - ORIGINAL MOTION PICTURE SOUNDTRACK

(MCA Records CD DMCG 6112)
'Love Me Two Times' – Aerosmith perform a spirited version of the old Doors classic, for the soundtrack of the ill fated Mel Gibson movie.

LOVE IN AN ELEVATOR CD SINGLE

(Original release 1989;
Geffen GEF 63CD)
Featuring 'Ain't Enough'. Although this track didn't make 'Pump' (due presumably to its similarity to 'Young Lust') it's still a fantastic up tempo rock song, full of innovative melody lines and a gorgeous Arabic sounding middle section. Worth rooting around for.

LIVIN' ON THE EDGE CD SINGLE

(Original release 1993;
Geffen GFSTD35)
This CD single features the previously unreleased 'Don't Stop'. Insistent, high powered rock'n'roll, it's somewhat let down by a formulaic 'rock' chorus, and more than a passing resemblance to a certain Def Leppard song.

EAT THE RICH CD SINGLE

(Original release 1993; Geffen
GEF GFSTD46)
Another CD single, backed with the previously unreleased 'Head First'. With its mellow, Yardbirds influenced groove, it could easily have replaced the dodgy 'Flesh' on 'Get a Grip'. Nice cover too.

THE OTHER SIDE
CD SINGLE
(Original release 1990;
Geffen GEF 79CD 7599-21614-2)
Includes Matt Dike's innovative reworking of 'The Other Side' - his honky tonk mix, imbuing a rather workmanlike rocker with a 90's country feel. Also present is a live version of the TV theme tune to 'Wayne's World', taken from Aerosmith's appearance on the show. 'Don't Forget To Wear A Rubber' advises Steven Tyler.

SHUT UP AND DANCE
CD SINGLE
(Original release 1994;
Geffen GEF GFSXD 75)
While 'Shut Up And Dance' is no 'Walk This Way', the supplementary tracks available on the disc include a satisfying, industrial remix of the 'Get A Grip' stalwart, 'Line Up' by the Butcher Bros, plus a gentle and evocative acoustic take of 'Crazy'.

JANIE'S GOT A GUN
(Original release 1989; 12" single
Geffen GEF 68 (T) A (7599-214160))
On the B-side of this single exists a smoking version of 'Rag Doll', recorded live at the Hershey Park Arena, Philadelphia, USA. Tyler is in particularly fine form.

NINE LIVES

As this book went to press, Aerosmith's latest studio album *Nine Lives* (the first to re-unite them with former labelmates Columbia/Sony) is still being mixed, and therefore cannot be included for review. That said, some tantalising tales concerning the making of the LP have surfaced, giving a clear indication that the 'Nine Lives' birthing process has been fraught with creative difficulties, internal strife and at times, downright hostility.

Since work began in January 1996, Aerosmith have sacked their manager of 12 years, Tim Collins (replacing him with new gun Wendy Laister), fired then re-hired sixth ear John Kalodner and released original choice of producer Glen 'Alanis Morissette' Ballard in favour of Kevin 'Silverchair' Shirley. If that weren't enough, it has also been alleged that Steven Tyler has once again lapsed into drug use (Tyler vociferously denies the accusations), sticksman Joey Kramer has had real difficulties with drum parts – his timing supposedly shot by years of cocaine abuse – (also denied) and that the group, following a protracted period of in-fighting, have revisited the fabled Steps Drug Rehabilitation Centre for a "conflict resolution week" (no denials here). To make matters even more embarrassing, the music press actually got hold of a letter sent to Tyler by his fellow band mates before their sabbatical stating that unless he modified his attitude he'd find himself a solo artist! Conflict resolution indeed.

Six months behind schedule, *Nine Lives* is released on March 18, 1997. Whether it proves to be a masterpiece or a dog is uncertain, but one thing remains clear – not since *Draw The Line* in 1977 has the making of an Aerosmith album drawn so much heat.

Acknowledgements and thanks to: Chris Charlesworth, *Rolling Stone*, *Guitar World*, *Creem*, *Pandora's Box* and, of course, Aerosmith.

INDEX